KT-569-936

THE
MEMSAHIB'S
COOKBOOK

To
Amanda

With lots of love
Mum & Dad
x x x.
Christmas 1990.

THE MEMSAHIB'S

COOKBOOK

Recipes from the Days of the Raj

RHONA AITKEN

PIATKUS

To Gordon, James, Susan, Lianne and Marion.

Thanks to Liz Bointon
for allowing me to use her
personal cookbooks and memories.

© 1989 Rhona Aitken text and illustrations

First published in 1989 by
Judy Piatkus (Publishers) Limited
of 5 Windmill Street, London W1

British Library Cataloguing in Publication Data
Aitken, Rhona
    The memsahib's cookbook
    I. Title
    641.5

ISBN 0–86188–885–5

Edited by Susan Fleming
Designed by Paul Saunders

Typeset by Phoenix Photosetting, Chatham, Kent
Printed and bound in Great Britain by Richard Clay Ltd, Bungay, Suffolk

CONTENTS

INTRODUCTION

THE *Memsahibs* were the wives of men serving in India, Ceylon and elsewhere in the tropical subcontinent. Throughout the years of the British Raj, stretching roughly from the mid nineteenth century up to the 1940s, these women gave of themselves to their adopted countries, many forfeiting the lives of their children, their husbands, parents and friends. Many were extraordinarily brave, living through the horrors of siege and massacre, some actually losing their own lives. The history of the Memsahibs is a remarkable one, and I have only been able to outline it briefly. However, one aspect of their lives – the major subject of this book – is the part they played in creating an Anglo–Indian cuisine, a cuisine which is unique in culinary history.

I myself was a latter-day Memsahib, living, bringing up a family – and cooking – in Ceylon of the late 1940s and early 1950s. My husband was born in Ceylon of a Raj family, and it was his grandfather, Edward Hamilton Aitken, who became well known as the 'humorous naturalist' and essayist, EHA. EHA's works, as well known as Kipling's at the time, are largely forgotten now, but their style, wit and shrewd understanding of nature, both human and animal, deserve to be more widely appreciated.

So this is why I have interspersed the recipes with extracts from EHA's writings. This little book is an affectionate tribute to those Memsahibs who preceded me, and to EHA himself, of course, and I hope my 'spicy mixture' will please.

Rhona Aitken, May 1989

THE MEMSAHIBS

THE British had been founding trading posts in India since the 1600s, but it was not until the eighteenth century that the British East India Company began enlarging their influence and acquiring real political as well as trading power across virtually the whole of the subcontinent. There were few British women in India at this time – the men came out for military service, for adventure, or to make money, and thereafter returned home to put down roots, buy houses or estates, and raise families. Shortly after the Mutiny of 1857, however, when the British Crown assumed government of the Raj (from a Hindi word meaning 'to rule'), the Suez Canal was opened in 1869. This considerably shortened the voyage time from Britain to India – which had once taken as long as six months round the Cape – to about three or four weeks, and more and more families began to be based in the subcontinent. The Memsahib had truly arrived.

What she encountered was a largely male society which had adapted, as men tend to do, to the status quo. Most had become accustomed to the heat and way of life, had become ardent curry enthusiasts, and all accepted without question the serried ranks of servants who saw, in some form or another, to the *Sahib*'s every need. What she also encountered was heat, dirt, insects, snakes, unfamiliar foods and ingredients, new and unfamiliar cultures, homesickness and, very probably, loneliness.

The Memsahibs have often been portrayed as petulant and spoiled, bullying down-trodden staff by day and indulging in infidelities and intrigues by night. Most Memsahibs were actually very ordinary and probably sheltered young ladies who, however well they might have mentally and physically prepared themselves for it, were faced with a completely alien environment. From a simple existence in Bradford or Bournemouth, they were plunged into the babel of Bombay; after a world of gentle walks to the village shop in the cool of an English morning, or teas by the fire at four, they were subjected to temperatures of nearly 100°F, dust, disease-bearing mosquitoes, and the knowledge that thousands of miles separated them from most of those they loved, and all with which they were familiar.

These Memsahibs – the women who were or became the wives of soldiers, tea and coffee planters, traders, civil servants – were drawn from all classes of British society, many of them sisters, poorer or younger relations, or friends of those already in India. Some girls came out as governesses or nannies, and some, like Adela Quested in E. M. Forster's *A Passage to India*, came to visit before marrying a man serving in India.

> 'Although Miss Quested had known Ronny well in England, she felt well advised to visit him before deciding to be his wife. India had developed sides of his character that she had never admired. His self-complacency, his censoriousness, his lack of subtlety, all grew vivid beneath a tropic sky.'

Some girls braved the voyage to India to seek the future husband who had proved so elusive at home. Sailings were announced in the newspapers, and all the young bachelors – as starved of (respectable) feminine company as the girls were of masculine – would go down to the docks to await their arrival. It was called the fishing fleet – because the girls were 'fishing' for husbands – but how humiliating it must have been for some to discover that the bait was not taken in India either . . .

Many Memsahibs were already wives, coming out with or to join their spouses. But whether the relationship was a long standing or relatively new one, an understanding husband – one who took time to explain and enlighten – might have given many Memsahibs a headstart in this alien land. Most wives would have been left to cope on their own, with the women's work that men think women 'know' automatically how to do. For what we think of as the golden age of the Memsahib was the age of the dominant male and the dependent female. She would have to mould herself to the needs of her husband, however difficult that might be. Far too many of the memoirs of the Memsahibs talk of the work that kept the *Sahib* busy and away from home from dawn to dusk, and of the consequent despair and loneliness of his wife.

The first problem would have been to adapt to the 'degree of destruction of this climate', and this is summed up very graphically by Emily Eden, sister of the Governor General of India in the late 1830s, in her letters home. However well the Memsahibs had ordered, bought and packed in the cool of England – 'a cargo of *large fans*; a *silver busk*, because

all steel busks become rusty and spoil the stay; night dresses with short sleeves, and net night-caps, because muslin is so hot' (*Miss Eden's Letters*) – they could not have anticipated the all-pervasive and invasive nature of the country's heat and wild life: lizards that scuttled up and down walls, snakes that sought the cool of the bathroom tiles, ducks that nested in the thunder-boxes, and insects which ate everything from photographs to books and her dresses.

> '. . . there is something ingenious in the manner in which the climate and the insects contrive to divide the work. One cracks the bindings of the books, the other eats up the inside; the damp turns the satin gown itself yellow, and the cockroaches eat up the net that trims it; the heat splits the ivory of a miniature, and the white maggots eat the paint; and so they go on helping each other and never missing anything!' (*Miss Eden's Letters*)

Another problem would have been that of staff. After a maximum of two in Britain – a cook and a tweeny, say – a new household of ten to fifteen servants would have been rather daunting. In *Behind the Bungalow*, EHA lists the Boy, the Dog-Boy, the Butler, the *Ghorawallah* or *Syce* (groom), the Cook, the *Mussaul* (the man of lamps, polisher of knives and washer of plates), the *Hamal* (cleaner of furniture) and the *Chupprassee* (bodyguard – but who was also 'above all, an unequalled child's servant'; in this latter category, he also 'catches butterflies, skins birds, blows eggs and runs after tennis balls'). Not to mention the *Dhobie* (washerman – was it he who suffered the eponymous itch, or did he cause it?), the *Dirzee* (tailor, mender of clothes), the *Malee* (gardener), the *Bheestee* (water carrier), the *Gowlee* or *Doodwallah* (milkman), and various other miscellaneous *wallahs* too numerous to list.

Emily Eden wrote of her household:

> 'I have all my rooms shut up and made dark before I leave them, and go out into my passage, where I find my two tailors sitting cross-legged, making my gowns; the two Dacca embroiderers whom I have taken into my private pay working at a frame of flowers that look like paintings; Chance, my little dog, under his own servant's arm; a *Meter* with his broom to sweep the rooms, two bearers who pull the *punkahs* [ceiling fans]; a sentry to mind that none of these steal anything; and a *Jemadar* [chief servant] and four *Hurkurus* [postal runners] who are my particular attendants and follow me about wherever I go.' (*Miss Eden's Letters*)

Emily Eden, more properly to be described as a *Lady Sahib*, would stay in India for only five or six years. The ordinary Memsahibs, however, would have to stay for the duration, and learn, by trial and error, how to run such a household. Potential problems stemmed not only from the large number of servants, but from their caste and hierarchical systems: the water carrier, for instance, would only carry water from the source, it was not he who should fill a pot or water a plant. Thus it was very easy for even an experienced Memsahib to make a mistake, and, however small, it could cause great offence. As EHA said, 'I have read that the making of one English pin employed nine men, but it is a vain boast. The rudiments of division of labour are not understood in Europe. In this country every trade is a breed.'

In the heat, too, it would have been easy for the Memsahib to lose her temper over the apparent obtuseness of a servant. Most would accept the criticism, fair or unfair, shrugging their shoulders as only Indian servants can, but some might be forced to leave, and the foolish Memsahibs who caused such defection were not respected. EHA wrote of how essential it was to keep a loyal staff: 'A man who parts lightly with his servants will never have a servant worth retaining. At the morning conference in the market [of Boys], where masters are discussed . . . none holds so low a place as the Sahib who had had eleven butlers in twelve months.'

If relations were difficult at first – EHA records the Butler's despair on page 20 – they could be resolved once the servants had become accustomed to the ways of the Memsahib, and she to theirs, and many households kept the same retainers for years, running like an extended family. Indeed, if the servants were there to look after every need of the Sahib and Memsahib, so the latter would have to return the compliment in other ways, looking after the staff's general health and the welfare of their families – which were seemingly numberless. If it wasn't schoolbooks for someone's cousin's sister's son, it was a cow for an uncle's wife's brother.

The multitude of servants led to one of the main problems of the Memsahib's existence – she had nothing to do. There were no household chores to perform, as all were taken care of by the various *wallahs*. Even the dog and the horse would be looked after by their individual servants. Her children were too, and her fears for them must also have been dominant. If the climate was destructive to adults, it was even more so to fair-skinned children and babies, and the British cemeteries in India and Ceylon are tragically packed with little headstones recording the ends of tiny lives. Although in Victorian and Edwardian times it was common

for children to be looked after by nannies or maidservants, the Memsahib's alternative, the *Ayah*, could be a slight liability. Usually single women who slept in the nursery and looked after the child's every need, the *Ayahs* were hated by the other servants (because they often became so close to the lonely Memsahib, perhaps?), and they could have rather nasty habits. Some were thought to stop crying and induce peace with a little opium administered to the baby from under her fingernail. Normally, though, the *Ayahs* adored the children – as do all Indians – and many of the Memsahib's babies grew up to be extraordinarily spoiled. (There was an insufferable three-year-old in Ceylon who was carried around on a cushion!)

However most children, if they survived, did not stay long in the tropics, as they would be sent home to be educated. EHA was a rarity, being educated in India; his grandson, my husband, was sent back to boarding school in Britain at the tender age of five. As the sailings took three to four weeks, and long leaves were only about every four years, the Memsahibs would see little of their children after that age, and their loneliness would be compounded. (As indeed would that of their children, sent to boarding schools in a climate and existence unfamiliar to *them*, and to the holiday ministrations of unknown aunts, uncles and grandparents.)

Such separations were part and parcel of the Memsahib's way of life. She was separated from her home and friends in Britain, from her children once they were old enough, from friends in the subcontinent who could, with frightening speed, be struck fatally with malaria or cholera. She was often separated from her husband too, and not only during the day, for many men, depending on their profession, would have to travel through the country for a proportion of the year. Every summer families, husbands and wives and children, would be separated when the frailer members would be dispatched to the hills to escape the gruelling heat of the plains. In India, this meant Simla, a town 7,000 feet above the sea, and created entirely by the British. Emily Eden amusingly voiced what many Memsahibs must have felt when they arrived in Simla:

'No wonder I could not live down below! We were never allowed a scrap of air to breathe – now I come back to the air again, I remember all about it. It is a cool sort of stuff, refreshing, sweet, even apparently pleasant to the lungs.' (*Up the Country*)

However, it was the lack of any meaningful occupation for the majority of the Memsahibs that caused the most insidious damage, gradually leading to an ennui and lethargy that was almost like a disease. With

no shop windows to gaze into, few new magazines or books, no theatres, none of the variety of social life they were used to, many early Memsahibs would give themselves up to the heat and to indolence lying about in darkened rooms all day, foregoing even the cool early-morning rides and the afternoon's embroidery before the evening's social events. They would gradually go into decline, and they packed the cabins of home-bound ships in efforts to recover their health. Some took to drink, some went mad, and some even took their own lives. Many, of course – and this is the subject of Anglo–Indian stories and novels from *The Circle* by Somerset Maugham to *Heat and Dust* by Ruth Prawer Jhabvala – sublimated their boredom by having affairs, and this is how the reputation of the Memsahibs deteriorated. For a lonely wife, perhaps one who did not know her husband too well – a dashing young subaltern, a handsome Rajah, or even just a homesick clerk – plus the heat, the earthiness (sensuality, even) of India, all conspired together.

In *Woman in India*, published in 1895, Mary Frances Billington wrote that it is only a strong character 'that does not become demoralised into flabbiness and inertia under the combined influences of heat, laziness, and servants at command. . . . The first sign of deterioration is when a woman omits her corsets from her toilette, and begins lolling about in a sloppy and tumbled tea-gown.' A Memsahib in Flora Annia Steel's 1893 novel, *Miss Stuart's Legacy*, put it more strongly: 'India is an ogre, eating us up body and soul, ruining our health, our tempers, our morals, our manners, our babies.'

However, many Memsahibs were able to cope with all that India offered, and learned to love the people and the country, often coming closer than their husbands to the heart of the culture and of India itself. EHA's wife obviously had no such problems – apart from that of the *Dirzee*(?):

> 'If she could only do without him, she would send him about his business and be the happiest woman in the world, for she could devote the whole day to music and painting and the improvement of her mind.'

In general, the more energetic Memsahibs would have spent their days writing letters, giving lessons, organising missionary and community work, attending sewing circles, helping out with the babies at the local hospitals, and drinking tea and coffee with friends. Many painted in oils and watercolour, and there are a wealth of painting collections, mainly of landscapes, fauna and flora, which are the work of Memsahibs over the many years the Britrish were in India. Charlotte Canning, wife of

another Governor General of India, at the time of the Mutiny, quieted her considerable and justified fears by painting, and her work was later admired by John Ruskin, the art historian, as 'the grandest representation of flowers he had ever seen'.

Many Memsahibs, particularly those of the late nineteenth and early twentieth centuries, would have been interested in cooking – although this was frowned upon to a large extent. The 'kitchen' would not normally be a place where any Memsahib would be expected to spend her time: in general it was simply a separate area, often outside under an awning, with a charcoal or wood-burning stove, sometimes a splendid iron affair called a Dover stove, often just a clay container. The heat produced was quite considerable, not to mention the sparks that showered out of its ever-open fire door. It was open because to close it meant cutting the wood into small pieces; it was much easier for the kitchen boy to put in logs two to three feet long and periodically push them into the stove with his strong toes. If the wood had not been dried properly, the smoke would be thick and choking, and it was no wonder that the early Memsahibs in their heavy billowing clothes were disinclined to get too close. (I myself cooked in such a 'kitchen' in the late 1940s – letting the side down rather, even at that late date – and spitting wood and charcoal peppered my skirts with a plethora of tiny burns. My toes also received a benison from time to time.)

Neither could many of the Memsahibs become involved in anything like menu planning or shopping. These were always the duty of the Cook. He would arrive early in the morning with his proposed menus for the day and a list of his requirements. On his return he would present a detailed list of his expenditure and receive payment. He made a 'little on the side' – in fact he would be *expected* to, one of his perks. Should the perks exceed the bounds of normality, a gentle 'Cook, would you just check this again, perhaps your arithmetic is not too accurate today' would probably be enough to elicit 'Oh Memsahib, this very hot weather, it affects the brain, I think. It was not 6 rupees but 6 annas for the plantains. What a foolish fellow I am.' As long as the weather was to blame, all was well. Above all, he must not lose face. Anyway, should he not get this perk from the market, it would be extracted from the Memsahib in other ways. Far better to let Cook do the shopping.

And with so many ingredients that would be entirely unfamiliar, no wonder. And no wonder either that the early cuisine of the Raj was considered fairly poor. The Memsahibs attempted to introduce the Anglo–French cuisine so prevalent at home – there are stories of mashed potato dyed and sculpted into chicken and fish shapes by enthusiastic Indian

cooks – but with the lack of many essential ingredients, it was impossible to achieve to a large extent. (The curries to which their husbands had so taken, were banished to Sunday *tiffin* or lunch). E. M. Forster, in *A Passage To India*, describes the menu at the Club:

> 'Julienne soup full of bullety bottled peas, pseudo-cottage bread, fish full of branching bones, pretending to be plaice, more bottled peas with the cutlets, trifle, sardines on toast: the menu of Anglo–India. A dish might be added or subtracted as one rose or fell in the official scale, the peas might rattle less or more, the sardines and the vermouth be imported by a different firm, but the tradition remained: the food of exiles, cooked by servants who did not understand it.'

However critical this might appear, it was quite amazing that so many servants, let alone cooks, *were* able to adapt, as EHA noted of butlers (see page 20). It always impressed me how Indian cooks would be able to rustle up a delicious meal from apparently nothing in a matter of moments. (There were mistakes, of course – one cook apparently gathered that he was to boil the *foie gras* and chill the asparagus!)

The majority of foodstuffs the Memsahibs wanted to have served and cooked would have to be imported in some form or another: tins of fish, fruit, cream and butter (the latter perhaps more acceptable than that offered by the *Doodwallah*, see page 111); bottled vegetables; and yeast which had to be sent by parcel post from Bombay and thus was never quite as fresh as it should be.

'Making do' or 'making the best of it' would have been the attitude at first – although some Anglo–Indian dishes became and remain classics – but gradually the Memsahibs learned, over the decades, to utilise the meats, fruits and vegetables of the country, adapting the basic recipes she would have written down for the cook to follow. Gradually he, too, learned to adapt the recipes of the Memsahibs to his own way of cooking and in return he taught the latter-day Memsahibs how to use spices, spice mixtures, chutneys, and the varying produce of his country.

It is the records of these lessons, the handwritten and printed collections of recipes of Memsahibs of the late nineteenth and early twentieth centuries, that I have plumbed for the selection here. Some of the dishes I used myself (and still do); many have come from my mother-in-law's cookbooks of the 1930s; and more from older cookbooks lent to me by old friends who lived in India before the 1930s or who had cookbooks left to them. They are a fascinating legacy of a unique way of life, and in themselves offer a slice of both British and culinary history.

COOK'S TIPS

I HAVE given what I consider to be a medium amount of spices in all these recipes. There are no hard and fast rules though, so you can change the amounts yourself with impunity (despite the quote below). I seldom mention salt and pepper for the same reason. In most of the recipes, ground spices are used. As a family we are fond of crunching through coriander seeds and cardamom pods. You may like to do the same.

Coconut

The coconut I use is the 7 oz (200 g) block of coconut cream. (Dunne River is the best, in my opinion.) If it is very hard, it should be cut into small pieces, but usually half an hour in a warm kitchen will soften it enough to be 'spooned'. Either way, it can be added to other, *wet*, ingredients (it would burn if heated dry). If a liquid is required, melt pieces in a little boiling water.

To make coconut milk, use fresh grated or dried flaked or desiccated coconut (*un*sweetened): soak in double its volume of boiling water for at least 30 minutes, and press the flesh well through a sieve (keep flesh for garnishing or for the recipe on page 94). You can also make coconut milk with the coconut cream, and a tinned milk is available which is much richer than 'home-made'.

Tamarind

Tamarind is sold in blocks. Pieces may be torn off and the pulp released (the only edible part) by soaking in boiling water for at least 20–30 minutes (you could leave it overnight). Break up the block with a spoon or your fingers (once the water is cool), to separate pods, seeds etc. Then sieve, pushing through as much pulp as possible, leaving behind seeds and pods which should be discarded. The resultant 'juice' is thick, more like a purée. The proportions should be in the region of 4 oz (100 g) tamarind to ¼ pint (150 ml) boiling water.

Tamarind is also sold as a concentrate in jars.

Yoghurt
A lot of plain yoghurt is used in the following recipes. When it is cooked, it tends to look very curdled. If you don't fancy this, and prefer a smooth sauce, dissolve 1 heaped tablespoon of flour in 4 tablespoons of either water, stock or yoghurt, and whisk into the curdled gravy.

Stock
Whenever stock is mentioned it would be best to use chicken. If you boil the bones every time you have a chicken, and strain the cool stock off into plastic bags and freeze them, you will always have a ready supply.

Eggs
Indian eggs are tiny, and a little by-line in one very old Indian cookbook announces that eleven village eggs weigh 6 oz (175 g)! I have adapted recipes to take account of our very much larger eggs.

Tomato Passata
I use a lot of tomato passata, which comes in packets rather like cartons of milk. It is 'creamed' tomatoes, offered by several major tomato-canning firms. If you can't find it – it tastes deliciously fresh – sieved canned tomatoes would be an acceptable substitute.

I can't resist a couple of final quotes from *Routledge's New Cookery Book*, published around the turn of the century. It is endearingly pompous!

> 'We object to a cook who would regulate the flavour of her dishes by her own taste; this arbitrary measure being offensive to delicacy and opposed to reason. What can be expected to be the result of such directions as "a squeeze of lemon", or "a good deal of salt or sugar"; thus leaving the whole nicety of the point of success to the caprice of the cook's palate.'

> 'Curries in the hot climate of India are an absolutely necessary stimulant to the relaxed system. The English currie is too often rendered nauseous by a careless adaptation of the seasoning. It must be particularly remembered that in India the currie, of whatever it may be composed, in only intended as a sauce or relish to the delicately boiled rice.'

EHA – THE HUMOROUS NATURALIST

Edward Hamilton Aitken – or EHA as he came to be known – was born in the Bombay Presidency of India in 1851. He was the son of Scottish missionaries, and, unlike most of his contemporaries, was educated in India. Taught at first by his father, he later graduated with an MA and a BA from Bombay University.

In 1870 he was appointed Latin Reader to the Deccan College at Poona, which accounts for his extensive knowledge of Latin classics, often quoted in his writings. He also read Greek – but that was for pleasure.

After six years in Poona he married, and entered the Customs and Salt Department of the Bombay Government. He was sent to take charge of the salt-*peons* at Kharagoda, and this was where EHA started to observe and record nature, in the village he called 'Dustypore'. First he described the 'Animal Surroundings of an Indian Bungalow' (in *Tribes on My Frontier*), then he tackled 'the Human Officials thereof, with their peculiarities, idiosyncrasies, and, to the European, strange methods of duty' (in *Behind the Bungalow*). Both these books, and another, *A Naturalist on the Prowl*, appeared first in the form of articles in the *Times* of India, before being collected into book form and published by Thacker, Spink & Co., Calcutta, and W. Thacker & Co., London.

In all these books, as Sir Philip Gosse wrote in *The London Mercury* of February 1933, 'was the same quality of truth, observation, and insight into the ways of animals, written in a simple, charming style, combined with a delightful, quiet sense of humour'. It was the latter quality which set him apart from other great naturalists such as W. H. Hudson, and it was even said that the humour bubbled through in his annual reports of the Customs Department of India, appearing like oases in an otherwise arid desert! He also wrote a field guide, *The Common Birds of Bombay*, the scholarship of which is interspersed with the same clear-sighted and nimble-penned grasp of character and habit in the avian world. Of the vulture, he says: 'That bald head and bare neck are not ornamental, but they mean business; they are the sleeves tucked up for earnest work'. And of the water wagtail, 'It follows the cattle in the pastures and runs in and out among their feet; they are its bearers, which drive the game for it'.

EHA also worked for the Customs on the frontier between Goa and North Kanara, a notorious hot-bed of malaria. He made very detailed investigations into the causes and often fatal ravages of the disease, and indeed discovered a new malaria-carrying mosquito which was christened, in his honour, *Anopheles aitkeni*.

In 1903 he was appointed Chief Collector of Customs and Salt Revenues at Karachi, and two years later he became District Gazetteer of Sind. EHA retired to Edinburgh shortly afterwards with his wife and five surviving children, but the drastic change of climate proved too much for him, and he died there of pneumonia on April 25th, 1909.

Throughout his life EHA was a keen naturalist, his principal concerns the animals, birds, reptiles and insects of India. However, he was also a shrewd observer of humanity, brown humanity, and *Behind the Bungalow* became an Anglo–Indian classic. EHA in his day was as famous as Rudyard Kipling in the subcontinent, but because he worked and lived only in India, his skill as an essayist was limited virtually to the Anglo–Indian community. Had he lived in England, he would have received the encouragement and appreciation due him – but of course, had he lived in England, he would never have written so acutely about the *Doodwallah*, the *Dhobie*, the hunting ant or the grey-winged bee . . .

A charming obituary in the *Journal* of the Bombay Natural History Society (of which he was a founder) reads as follows:

> 'He looked upon all creatures in the proper way; as if each had a soul and character of its own. He loved them all and was unwilling to hurt any of them, and accordingly was not a collector of specimens except in a very small way, just enough to get as thorough knowledge as he judged sufficient of their lives and habits.'

THE BUTLER

YOUR Boy looks after you, whereas your Butler looks after the other servants, and you look after him; at least I hope you do. From this it follows that the Boy flourishes only in the free atmosphere of bachelordom. If master marries, the Boy sometimes becomes a Butler, but I have generally seen that the change was fatal to him. He feels a share at first in master's happiness on the auspicious occasion, and begins to fit on his new dignity. He provides himself with a more magnificent *cumberbund*, enlarges the border of gold thread on his puggree, and furbishes up his English that he may converse pleasantly with *mem saheb*. He orders about the other servants with a fuller voice than before, and when anyone calls for a chair, he no longer brings one himself, but commands the *hamal* to do so. He feels supremely happy! Alas! before the *mem saheb* has been many weeks in the house, the change of air begins to disagree with him – not with his body, but with his spirit, and though he may bear up against it for a time, he sooner or later asks leave to go to his country. His new mistress is nothing loth to be rid of him, nor master either, for even his countenance is changed; and so the Butler's brief reign comes to an end, and he departs, deploring the unhappy match his master has made. Why could not so liberal and large-minded a *saheb* remain unmarried, and continue to cast the shadow of his benevolence on those who were so happy to eat his salt, instead of taking to himself a *madam*, under whom there is no peace night or day? As he sits with his unemloyed friends seeking the consolation of the never-failing

beeree, the ex–butler narrates her ladyship's cantankerous ways, how she eternally figeted over a little harmless dust about the corners of the furniture, as if it was not the nature of dust to settle on furniture; how she would have window panes washed which had never been washed before; her meanness in inquiring about the consumption of oil and milk and firewood, matters which the *saheb* had never stopped to look into; and her unworthy and insulting practice of locking up stores, and doling them out day by day, not to mention having the cow milked in her presence: all of which made him so ashamed in the presence of the other servants that his life became bitter, and he was forced to ask for his *ruzza*.

. . . "but the *sahebs* are better than the *mem sahebs*. The *sahebs* are hot and get angry sometimes, but under them a man can live and eat a mouthful of bread. With the *mem sahebs* it is nothing but worry, worry, worry. Why is this so dirty? Who broke that plate? When was that glass cracked? Alas! why do the *sahebs* marry such women?"   EHA

———————◆———————

DOMINGO, THE COOK

AND to Domingo the preparation of dinner is indeed a fine art. Trammel his genius, confine him within the limits of what is commonly called a "plain dinner," and he cannot cook. He stews his meat before putting it into a pie, he thickens his custard with flour instead of eggs, he roasts a leg of mutton by boiling it first and doing "littlee brown" afterwards; in short, what does he not do? . . . But let him loose on a *burra khana*, give him *carte blanche* as to sauces and essences and spicery, and all his latent faculties and concealed accomplishments unfold themselves like a lotus flower in the morning. . . . And the marvel increases when we

consider the simplicity of his implements and materials. His studio is fitted with half a dozen small fire-places and furnished with an assortment of copper pots, a chopper, two tin spoons – but he can do without these, – a ladle made of half a cocoanut shell at the end of a stick, and a slab of stone with a stone roller on it; also a rickety table, a very gloomy and ominous looking table, whose undulating surface is chopped and hacked and scarred, begrimed, besmeared, smoked, oiled, stained with juices of many substances. On this table he minces meat, chops onions, rolls pastry, and sleeps; a very useful table. In the midst of these he bustles about, putting his face at intervals into one of his fires and blowing through a short bamboo tube, which is his bellows, such a potent blast that for a moment his whole head is enveloped in a cloud of ashes and cinders, which also descend copiously on the half-made tart and the *soufflé* and the custard.   EHA

ONE OF DOMINGO'S MENUS
[plus translation]

Though Domingo is naturally shy, and does not make a display of his attainments, he is a man of education, and is quite prepared, if you wish it, to write out his *menu*. Here is a sample:

SOUP
Salary Soup [celery soup]

FIS
Heel Fish Fry [a fried fish of sorts]

MADISH
Russel Pups [rissoles]
Wormsil Mole [sole *mollé*]

JOINT
Roast Bastad [oh dear!]

TOAST
Anchovy Poshteg [poached egg and achovy]

PUDDIN
Billimunj [blancmange]
Ispunj rolli [sponge roll]

. . . I must take this opportunity to record a true story of a *menu*, though it does not properly pertain to Domingo, but an ingenious Ramaswamy, of Madras. This man's master liked everything very proper, and insisted on a written *menu* at every meal. One morning Ramaswamy was much embarrassed, for the principal dish at breakfast was to be devilled turkey. "Devil very bad word," he said to himself; "how can write?" At last he solved the difficulty, and the dish appeared as "D____d turkey".   EHA

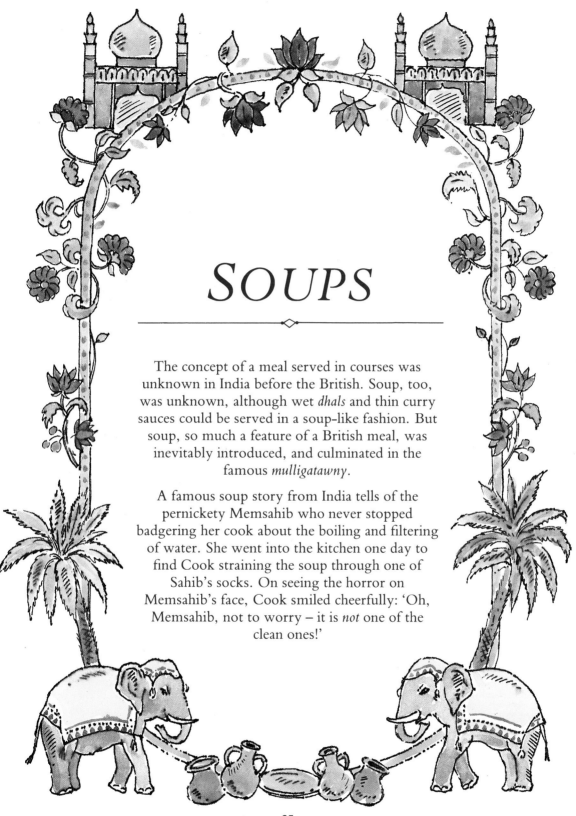

SOUPS

The concept of a meal served in courses was unknown in India before the British. Soup, too, was unknown, although wet *dhals* and thin curry sauces could be served in a soup-like fashion. But soup, so much a feature of a British meal, was inevitably introduced, and culminated in the famous *mulligatawny*.

A famous soup story from India tells of the pernickety Memsahib who never stopped badgering her cook about the boiling and filtering of water. She went into the kitchen one day to find Cook straining the soup through one of Sahib's socks. On seeing the horror on Memsahib's face, Cook smiled cheerfully: 'Oh, Memsahib, not to worry – it is *not* one of the clean ones!'

Ceylon Tapioca Soup

SERVES 6

Tapioca consists of pellets made from manioc or cassava flour (the roots are a staple in many parts of the Third World). In cooking, apart from nursery and invalid food associations, it is used as a soup or stew thickener rather like cornflour or arrowroot (indeed one of its names is Brazilian arrowroot).

◆

3 tablespoons tapioca
2 pints (1.2 litres) chicken stock
3 tablespoons dry sherry (more or less!)
1 teaspoon chopped fresh thyme
1 teaspoon chopped fresh marjoram
¼ teaspoon chilli powder
salt and freshly ground pepper

◆

Simmer the tapioca in 1½ pints (900 ml) of the stock for about half an hour.

In a small pan gently simmer the other ingredients in the remaining stock for 10–15 minutes. Sieve the liquid into the tapioca pan, and season to taste. Should the soup become too thick, simply add a little more stock or water.

Esau's Potage

SERVES 6

I have no idea of the provenance of this recipe, but it has been served at endless dinner parties. *Dhal*, or lentils, are central to Indian cuisine, and some wet, or runnier *dhal* dishes resemble thick soups, which perhaps eased their progress from vegetable dish to first-course soup status. Lentils were considered to be 'poor man's food', and to aid the digestion of the sick.

EHA records another use for *dhal*: 'Horses in this country are fed mostly on "gram", *cicer arietinum*, a kind of pea, which, when split, forms *dall*, and can be made into a most nutritious and palatable curry. The *Ghorawalla* [groom] recognises this fact. If he is modest, you may be none the wiser, perhaps none the worse; but if he is not, then his horse will grow lean, while he grows stout.'

◆

2 oz (50 g) lentils
3–4 oz (75–100 g) onion, finely chopped
1 garlic clove, crushed
1 teaspoon sugar
½ teaspoon curry powder or paste
½ oz (15 g) butter
2 pints (1.2 litres) stock
6 oz (175 g) potatoes, peeled and cubed
2 oz (50 g) long-grain rice
2 teaspoons vinegar
1 tablespoon chopped fresh parsely

◆

Gently sauté the lentils, onion, garlic, sugar and curry powder in the butter for a few minutes, then add the stock. Simmer for half an hour.

Add the potato, rice, vinegar and parsley. Simmer for a further 20–25 minutes. This is supposed to be a thick soup, but it is easy to adjust with extra potato or stock.

THE DOUBTING MEMSAHIB

A LADY was inveighing to a friend against the whole race of Indian cooks as dirty, disorderly, and dishonest. She had managed to secure the services of a Chinese cook, and was much pleased with the contrast. Her friend did not altogether agree with her, and was sceptical about the immaculate Chinaman. "Put it to the test," said the lady; "just let us pay a visit to your kitchen, and then come and see mine." So they went together. What need to describe the *Bobberjee-Khana*? They glanced around, and hurried out, for it was too horrible to be endured long. When they went to the Chinaman's kitchen, the contrast was indeed striking. The pots and pans shone like silver; the table was positively sweet; everything was in its proper place, and Chang himself, sitting on his box, was washing his feet in the soup tureen!   EHA

Mulligatawny Soup

SERVES 6–8

'Pepper water' was the nearest thing to soup in the cuisine of India, and indeed the word mulligatawny comes from the Tamil words *molegoo* (pepper) and *tunes* (water). It was originally a vegetarian 'sauce', but the British added meat and various other ingredients to create a variety of mulligatawnies which were popular in India and Ceylon, but had an extremely bad press back home in England!

The soup below is one which our delightful cook in Ceylon, Soloman, used to serve us in huge Victorian soup bowls. A basic peppered water was flavoured with various other ingredients, then the soup would be served with side bowls of cooked rice, lime wedges, grated coconut, snippets of fried bacon, quartered hard-boiled eggs and sliced chillies. You helped yourself to what you wanted – a meal in itself.

◆

2½ pints (1.8 litres) stock
7 oz (200 g) coconut cream, cut into chunks
1 heaped teaspoon each ground cumin and coriander
1 teaspoon chilli powder (flat or heaped!)
1 small tin tomato purée

Flavouring ingredients
1–2 onions, chopped and fried in butter until brown
2 tablespoons chutney juice
a few cardamom seeds, lightly crushed
salt and freshly ground pepper

◆

Simmer all the basic soup ingredients together for 15 minutes, then add all or any of the flavouring ingredients to make the soup exactly as you like it. Serve hot with side dishes as described above.

STINK-BUGS

TAKING first place in order of unmitigated nauseousness, . . . a single individual [stink-bug] is most impressive when it is crushed or tumbles into scalding soup.

. . . I knew a promising young man who took one in his soup!

I have felt ever since that I could give any price for a Book of Manners that would tell what a gentleman at a dinner-party should do under such circumstances. EHA

Chicken Broth with Lady's Fingers

SERVES 6

The long, slim green vegetable called okra, or *bindhi* in India, was named lady's fingers by the Memsahibs (for obvious reasons). When sliced, the five- to six-sided circles look very pretty, and their glutinous qualities make for good soup. Other famous okra dishes are the Creole *gumbo* and West Indian *callaloo*. In India, okra is used as a thickener and binder, and for medicinal purposes.

2 pints (1.2 litres) good chicken stock
1 large old potato, peeled and cubed
2 bay leaves
2 chilli peppers, de-seeded and chopped (optional)
8 oz (225 g) lady's fingers, thinly sliced in rings

Garnish
2 rashers lean bacon, crisp fried and chopped
2 tablespoons fresh chopped parsley

Simmer all the ingredients, except the lady's fingers, together for 15 minutes.

Add the lady's fingers and simmer for another 15 minutes. Taste a green ring, which should be tender. If the lady's fingers are a little older than we might like after their travels this far around the world, simmer them a little longer.

If you use tinned okra, I suggest you snip them into pieces with scissors as they tend to squash when you use a knife. These are already cooked, of course, so only need to be heated through in the stock.

Spinach Soup with Cream and Egg

SERVES 6

 Spinach grows all over India and Ceylon, often in the wild, and it is very popular, being used in soups and sauces as well as in vegetable and meat dishes. The Asian version has rather more flavour than the European and tastes almost like sorrel.

---

1 lb (450 g) spinach, finely chopped or puréed
1 heaped teaspoon cornflour
½ teaspoon freshly grated nutmeg
2 pints (1.2 litres) stock
salt and freshly ground pepper

Garnish
¼ pint (150 ml) double cream, semi-whipped
4 hard-boiled eggs, whites and yolks grated separately

Cook spinach briefly in as little water as possible. When cool, work in the cornflour and nutmeg. Add the stock and simmer for 10 minutes. Season at this stage if you wish.

Pour into individual soup bowls and pour a swirl of cream into each. Sprinkle a patch of egg white and a patch of egg yolk over each bowl and serve at once.

As it will take you a little time to add the cream and egg, do make sure your soup bowls are really hot before adding the soup.

FIRST COURSES

At the Memsahib's dinner parties, first courses or
starters would normally consist of little fish dishes
(simply smaller versions of main-course dishes),
or the constant staples of her store-cupboard –
tinned salmon, sardines or anchovies. These
would be served on toast, or in soufflés or
mousses.

Eggs were always plentiful – from all those
scrawny little chickens – but their provenance and
age were not always to be trusted. EHA's
Domingo had a way with them – and with
hygiene (see page 36).

Prawns Mantalini

SERVES 4

 This recipe comes from a personal cookery book of 1913. Who Mantalini was, I have no idea. The prawns used would be a sweet, freshwater variety.

◆

4 rounds white bread
a little oil
8 stuffed olives
30 capers, drained
4 anchovy fillets
2 oz (50 g) butter
8 large prawns or 24–28 small ones

Garnish
cucumber matchsticks

◆

Cut your slices of bread into attractive shapes (circles, triangles, or use a biscuit cutter). Fry until crisp and golden in a little oil, then drain well on kitchen paper.

Chop the olives, capers and anchovy finely and mix into 1½ oz (40 g) of the butter. Spread this thick paste on to the fried bread.

Melt the remaining butter in a frying pan and when sizzling, toss in the prawns, then pile on to the savoury toasts. Serve with a small heap of cucumber matchsticks.

Norwegian Panna

SERVES 4

This recipe was produced by our little bandy-legged cook, Apuhamie. He must have acquired it through the cooks' 'grapevine'. It is a surprisingly good pâté, that is much tastier than it sounds.

---

8 oz (225 g) spinach, chopped
3 oz (75 g) butter
2 garlic cloves, crushed
2 hard-boiled eggs, peeled
1 tin sardines (reserve the oil)
1 tin anchovies (reserve the oil)

Gently cook the spinach in half the butter, being careful not to overcook and so lose the lovely green colour.

Combine all the other ingredients, including the remaining butter, in a blender. Add the cooled spinach and blend again, adding some of the reserved fish oils if it appears to be too stiff.

Fill individual ramekins and chill for an hour or so in the fridge. This improves the consistency and the flavour. Serve with crusty bread.

EHA on Eggs

THEN he [Domingo] takes up an egg, gives it three smart raps with the nail of his forefinger, and in half a second the yoke [sic] is in one vessel and the white in another. The fingers of his left hand are his strainer. Every second or third egg he tosses aside, having detected, as it passed through the said strainer that age had rendered it unsuitable for his purposes; sometimes he does not detect this. From eggs he proceeds to onions, then he is taking the stones out of raisins, or shelling peas. There is a standard English cookery book which commences most of its instructions with the formula, "wash your hands carefully, using a nail brush." Domingo does not observe this ceremony, but he often wipes his fingers upon his pantaloons. EHA

Eggs Mollet (Hot)

SERVES 3–6

 This dish was a great favourite in Ceylon, and it has a rich and satisfying flavour (brains were often served in the same way). With a green salad and a bowl of your own home-made chutney, it is a meal fit for a Rajah!

The name comes from the French culinary term for eggs boiled for 1½ minutes, then plunged into cold water, which makes for a set white but a yolk that is still fairly runny. Under the influence of the Memsahib and her cook, spice additions were inevitable.

Use either soft-boiled or poached eggs, counting on two eggs per person for a main course or one for a first course. Eggs Mollet may be served with toast, but rice is the best accompaniment. Simply boil some and arrange in a ring on a hot plate.

◆

6 eggs, cooked (see above) and shelled
6 oz (175 g) rice, freshly cooked

Sauce
8 oz (225 g) onion, thinly sliced
3 tablespoons oil
1 small tin tomato purée
4 oz (100 g) coconut cream, broken into pieces
1 tablespoon fresh lime or lemon juice
3 tablespoons chutney juice
½ teaspoon each of ground coriander and cumin
¼ teaspoon allspice powder
½ pint (300 ml) water

◆

For the sauce, fry the onion in the oil until golden brown. When it smells quite delicious, add all the other ingredients and mix well. If it appears too thick, add a little extra water. Allow the sauce to bubble for 5 minutes to allow the flavours to combine and grow.

Place the cooked eggs in the centre of the rice ring, and pour over the sauce. This is sufficient to heat your eggs without overcooking them.

Eggs Mollet (Cold)

SERVES 3–8

 This has a strong flavour which can easily be altered to your own particular taste. Less mayonnaise and more cream both make a lovely sauce, but you will find that unless you use double cream, it will be too thin. Rice makes a good accompaniment, but rice to be served cold is nicer when cooked a little bit longer than rice to be served hot.

6–8 eggs, cooked as on page 37, cooled and shelled
rice as on page 37

Sauce
¼ pint (150 ml) mayonnaise
½ pint (300 ml) double cream
2 oz (50 g) tomato purée
2 tablespoons apricot jam, sieved
2 teaspoons curry paste (use ½ teaspoon for a non-hot mollet)
2 teaspoons lime or lemon juice

Garnish
2 tablespoons snipped fresh chives

Simply mix the sauce ingredients together. Arrange the cold eggs on the cold rice, and spoon the sauce over. Sprinkle with the chives.

THE MUSSAUL,
OR MAN OF LAMPS

WHEN the Mussaul has disposed of the breakfast things . . . he betakes himself to the great work of the day, the polishing of the knives. He first plunges the ivory handles into boiling water, and leaves them to steep for a time, then . . . arranging a plank of wood in a sloping position, holds it fast with his toes, rubs it well with a piece of bath brick, and commences to polish with all the energy which he has saved by the neglect of other duties. . . . As you listen to that baleful sound, you seem to feel with your finger points the back of each good, new knife getting sharper and sharper, and to watch its progress as it wears away at the point of greatest pressure, until the end of the blade is connected with the rest by a narrow neck, which eventually breaks, and the point falls off, leaving the knife in that condition so familiar to us all, when the blade, about three inches long, ends in a jagged, square point, the handle having, meanwhile, acquired a rich orange hue. Oh, those knives! those knives!   EHA

FISH DISHES

With thousands of miles of coastline it is not surprising that the Indians eat a lot of fish. However, the Memsahibs who settled inland would have had trouble finding it fresh, so salted and dried would have been a staple. Bombay duck is the classic example (see page 125). It was apparently due to the British that fishing for crustacea such as prawns and shrimps was introduced to the subcontinent. The old cookbooks mention two fish only, the seer and pomfret. The former is described by Mrs Beeton as 'not unlike the salmon, but its flesh is white,' and the latter is a large flat sea fish, occasionally available here now. Everything apart from those two they simply call 'fish'. Therefore, virtually any fish can be used in most of the following recipes.

Fish and Coconut

SERVES 4

Coconut makes a wonderful accompaniment for fish. Its use is commonplace in the south, but virtually unknown in the north.

4 fish fillets
2 garlic cloves
1 teaspoon ground cumin
1 teaspoon ground coriander
½ teaspoon ground turmeric
¼ teaspoon chilli powder
7 oz (200 g) onions, thinly sliced
2 oz (50 g) olive oil
2 oz (50 g) butter
4 oz (100 g) coconut cream, dissolved in ¼ pint (150 ml) hot water

Put the fish fillets on a plate and rub the garlic, cumin, coriander, turmeric and chilli into them.

Fry the onion in half the oil, and when brown, place on a plate. Add the rest of the oil and the butter to the pan and fry the fish fillets for a few minutes. Place them with the onions.

Pour the coconut and water into the frying pan. Allow to bubble for a minute or two, then carefully return the fish and onion. Simmer just enough to heat the fish through. Serve at once.

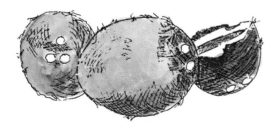

Fish with Fresh Lime Sauce

SERVES 4

 Yoghurt is used a lot in Indian cookery, especially in the north, and was probably originally made with buffalo milk. The Memsahibs would not have encountered it before, but would have welcomed the flavour it gave to dishes of rice, meat and fish alike.

1½ lb (675 g) plaice fillets

Sauce
1 tablespoon plain flour
juice of 2 limes
½ teaspoon ground turmeric
1 tablespoon chopped fresh mint
10 oz (275 g) plain yoghurt

Combine the flour, lime juice, turmeric and mint, and mix into the yoghurt. Allow to stand for about half an hour if possible, to develop the full flavour.

Grill the plaice fillets for a few minutes on each side. Bring the yoghurt sauce to boiling point. Pour over the fillets and serve at once.

Fillets of Fish Claudine

◇

SERVES 4

This recipe came from my mother-in-law's cookbook, dated 1913, but who Claudine was, I have no idea!

◆

4 fillets of meaty fish (sole, plaice, monkfish, haddock,
whiting or coley), skinned
the juice of 2 limes
4 fl oz (110 ml) olive oil, or ½ olive oil and ½ sunflower oil
1 medium onion, very thinly sliced
1 fat garlic clove, crushed

Sauce
7 oz (200 g) onions, chopped
2 tablespoons capers, chopped
1 teaspoon ground coriander
8 stuffed green olives, chopped
8 anchovy fillets, chopped
1 oz (25 g) butter
1 tablespoon plain flour
½ pint (300 ml) milk

◆

Immerse the fish in a marinade made from the lime juice, olive oil, onion and garlic. Leave for at least an hour, turning at least once.

Take the fish out. Dry it and put on a plate. Strain the lumps out of the marinade and allow the strained oil and lime juice to settle in a small bowl or jug so that you can skim some of the oil off the top. Lightly fry the fish in a little of this oil when you have made the sauce.

For the sauce, fry the chopped onion in a little of the oil from the marinade, then add the capers, coriander, olives and anchovies.

Melt the butter in a small pan. Add the flour and cook for 1 minute. Add the milk and cook until thickened. Add the caper mixture to the white sauce. The remaining lime juice may be added if liked.

Pour the sauce over the fried fish. Place in a moderately hot oven at 375°F/190°C/gas 5 for a few minutes just to ensure it is nice and hot, and serve with mashed potato and peas or beans.

LIZARDS

ONE peculiar feature of life in India is the way we are beset by lizards, and nobody seems to notice it. We all come out to this country more or less prepared to find scorpions in our slippers, snakes twined about our hair, and white ants eating up the bed in one night, so that in the morning we are lying on the floor; but nobody warns us to expect red-throated hobgoblins clambering about the trellis, and snaky green lizards prying about the verandah at noonday, and little geckos visiting the dinner-table at night.   EHA

Kedgeree

SERVES 4

Kedgeree was originally a lentil and rice dish, but it was the British Army in India who first adopted it as a rice-only breakfast dish, adorning it with fish, probably dried or salted. It is an accommodating dish, and it can be made in several different ways. The most popular way today is with smoked haddock (unavailable in the days of the Memsahibs). However a 1928 recipe extols tinned salmon, while a magazine from 1964 uses fresh salmon. This Ceylon recipe is very plain, not all that highly spiced, and was taken from a handwritten 1930s cookbook.

1 lb (450 g) smoked haddock
½ pint (300 ml) milk, plus a little extra
10 oz (275 g) long-grain rice
3 hard-boiled eggs, chopped

Sauce
2 oz (50 g) butter
1 heaped tablespoon plain flour
½ teaspoon ground turmeric

Simmer the fish in the milk for 5 minutes. Strain the milk into a jug, and flake, skin and bone the fish.

Cook the rice. Combine the fish, rice and chopped egg in a large casserole. Cover and keep warm in a moderate oven, 350°F/180°C/ gas 4, until you have made the sauce.

Melt the butter in the pan, add the flour and turmeric, and cook for a minute or two. Slowly add the milk from the fish, using more if need be to thin it down. Stir well and simmer for 5–10 minutes.

Serve the sauce and rice separately, and to make the kedgeree more interesting, add some little side dishes of grilled bacon snippets, chopped sweet peppers, chopped parsley mixed with diced un-peeled cucumber and/or mango chutney.

Kidgeree

This is taken word for word from a cookbook printed in 1919, *Rout-ledge's New Cookery Book*, edited by Anne Bowman.

 'Kidgeree is chiefly used as a breakfast dish, especially on maigre days. Boil the rice as for a curry, and when dry put it into a stew-pan, and add an equal quantity of fried sole or whiting, raised from the bone in neat fillets, 2 oz butter, a good seasoning of salt, Cayenne and black pepper; stir the whole over the fire until thoroughly heated – then beat two eggs, stir them in and serve the whole immediately hot, in a silver dish.

Any scallops of cold fish can be used, and a few shrimps are an improvement. In India the green chilli is introduced as seasoning.'

Kedcheree

This recipe appeared in *Gre-Fydd's Family Fare*, sub-titled *The Young Housewife's Daily Assistant*, published in 1874. The kedcheree was served, according to a later English cookbook, with little pieces of veal dipped first in beaten egg and then in curry powder, then fried in butter.

 'Wash half a pint of split peas, and boil them for two hours and a half in a quart of water; add half a pound of rice (well washed) and continue to boil for twenty-five minutes, stirring frequently to keep it from burning.

Chop three onions and fry them in butter (6 ounces) till slightly browned; drain off the water, add the peas and the rice to the onions; season with a teaspoonful of salt, a quarter of a saltspoonful of cardamoms, the eighth part of a nutmeg, grated. Stir and fry until all the butter is absorbed and the whole is of a pale brown colour.'

THE DOG-BOY

IN Bombay it is not enough to fit yourself with a Boy: your dog requires a Boy too. I have always felt an interest in the smart little race of Bombay dog-boys. As a corps, they go on with little change from year to year, but individually they are of short duration, and the question naturally arises, What becomes of them all when they outgrow their dog-boyhood? From such observations as I have been able to make, I believe the dog-boy is not a species by himself, but represents the early, or larva, stage of several varieties of domestic servants. The clean little man, in neat print jacket and red velveteen cap, is the young of a butler; while another, whom nothing can induce to keep himself clean, would probably, if you reared him, turn into a *ghorawalla*. . . . Like all larvae, dog-boys eat voraciously and grow rapidly. You engage a little fellow about a cubit high, and for a time he does not seem to change at all; then one morning you notice that his legs have come out half a yard or more from his pantaloons, and soon your bright little page is a gawky, long-limbed lout, who comes to ask for leave that he may go to his country and get married. . . . At any rate, when once your boy begins to grow long and weedy, his days as a dog-boy are ended. He will pass through a chrysalis stage in his country, or somewhere else, and after a time emerge in his mature form, in which he will still remember you, and *salaam* to you when he meets you on the road.   EHA

Prawns in Coconut

SERVES 4

This is my own recipe which I developed while in Ceylon. There are many large prawns there, and they are quite delicious.

This dish makes a tasty starter served with big chunks of bread to mop up the lovely gravy. For a main course, serve with rice and sprinkle the top with chopped parsley and hard-boiled egg. Any other firm–fleshed fish can be cooked this way, monkfish for example.

---

1 onion, finely chopped
2 oz (50 g) butter
4 tomatoes, chopped
2 oz (50 g) coconut cream, cut into little pieces
½ teaspoon ground turmeric
½ teaspoon chilli powder
1 lime or lemon
1 lb (450 g) prawns, shelled

Gently fry the onion in the butter. Try not to allow it to get too brown, but make sure it is thoroughly cooked. When soft, add all the other ingredients apart from the prawns. Simmer for 5 minutes and then add the prawns for just long enough to heat them through, about 3 minutes. Don't overcook them as they go very hard.

The juice from the tomatoes plus the butter usually produces enough liquid to melt the coconut cream to a nice consistency, but if it seems to be too thick, just add a little water.

CHICKEN DISHES

The ancestor of all the chickens we rear and eat today was the Indian jungle fowl. At the time of the Memsahibs, the small and scrawny birds that scratched and pecked around every corner would have been the staple meat; if she were having it for dinner, she would probably have seen it running around at tea-time! So tough was it, that it required quite lengthy cooking (quite unnecessary with our present-day birds). Today in India, chicken is considered a luxury and its very name has become a metaphor for good living and affluence. It's an ideal meat for curries, however, as it is so quick and easy to cook. Always skin pieces before cooking.

Chicken Tamarind

SERVES 6

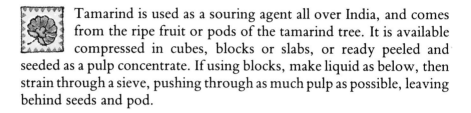
Tamarind is used as a souring agent all over India, and comes from the ripe fruit or pods of the tamarind tree. It is available compressed in cubes, blocks or slabs, or ready peeled and seeded as a pulp concentrate. If using blocks, make liquid as below, then strain through a sieve, pushing through as much pulp as possible, leaving behind seeds and pod.

---◆---

4 oz (100 g) tamarind pulp
¼ pint (150 ml) boiling water
2 medium onions, roughly 9 oz (250 g), sliced
4 tablespoons cooking oil
6 chicken breasts or joints, cut in half and skinned
1 teaspoon (or less) chilli powder
2 teaspoons each of ground cumin, coriander and cardamom
1½ teaspoons ground turmeric
4 oz (100 g) tinned coconut milk

---◆---

Cover the tamarind with the boiling water and leave on one side to become liquid.

Brown the onions in the oil, then add the pieces of chicken. Brown by turning once or twice. Add the spices and the coconut milk, and mix thoroughly. Strain the tamarind into the chicken, adding extra water if the dish seems too dry.

This can then be covered with foil or a lid and simmered on the stove or poured into a casserole, covered and placed in a moderately hot oven at 375°F/190°C/gas 5 for about half an hour.

THE MOSQUITO

WHY can they not bleed us painlessly? Why make us pay fees in anguish for the operation? It can be no advantage to them that we wince and jump when they sit down to dine. Who would thank anybody for inventing a pump which should tickle the earth so horribly as to bring on earthquakes whenever one went for water?

. . . mosquitos are always most venomous where they can scarcely ever have a chance of biting – in pestilential swamps and jungles inhabited by such impenetrable pachyderms as the wild elephant and the rhinoceros. Among rank weeds in deserted Bombay gardens, too, there is a large speckled, unmusical mosquito, raging and importunate and thirsty, which will give a new idea in pain to anyone that visits its haunts.

. . . And what is to be done? Well, by dusting and sweeping and burning incense . . . you can make them very unhappy and . . . you can make yourself utterly abominable to them by anointing your hands and face with toilet vinegar . . . But all means of prevention are more or less disappointing, for after all it is ordained that mosquitos shall bit us. EHA

Soloman's Chicken Hot-Pot

SERVES 4

 Soloman was our original cook in Ceylon, a wonderful old man who wore his hair in a bun with a comb, like a coronet around his head. His little helper was Apuhami who later took over the role.

This tasty dish was all in aid of 'how to enjoy a very tough old market chicken'. We, however, have the choice of using chicken joints, a jointed roaster or a jointed boiler. The latter will have a lovely flavour but will need to simmer for 1½ hours at least. If this seems a long time for a chicken, take heart – the original recipe cooks the poor old hen for 3½ hours!

---

4 lamb's kidneys, cleaned and sliced
1 chicken, jointed, or 4 chicken joints
3 medium onions, roughly 10–11 oz (275–300 g), chopped
5 tablespoons cooking oil
3½ oz (90 g) tomato purée (1 small tin)
2 bay leaves, crushed or cut into small pieces
2 teaspoons coriander seeds
½ teaspoon each of chilli powder, mixed spice, powdered cinnamon, freshly ground black pepper and freshly grated nutmeg
1 tablespoon fresh chopped thyme
4 large potatoes, peeled and sliced

Brown the kidney, chicken and onion in the oil. Place everything but the potato in a casserole, and mix well. Arrange the sliced potatoes neatly over the top. Barely cover with water and cook in the oven at 400°F/ 200°C/gas 6 for 60 minutes. Cover only if it seems necessary.

Sargeant's Chicken

SERVES 5

 This recipe – from a private cookbook – must have had an Army association. The original used slices of cooked chicken, no Chinese leaves and no lemon. It was also cooked for a lot longer – crisp vegetables were not the fashion then.

———◆———

3 oz (75 g) butter, plus a little extra
5 chicken breasts, skinned, each cut into four pieces
2 medium onions, roughly 9 oz (250 g), thinly sliced
2 leeks, white part only, thinly sliced
3 carrots, roughly 8 oz (225 g), cut into little matchsticks
4 oz (100 g) Chinese leaves, shredded
2 inch (5 cm) piece fresh ginger, peeled and thinly sliced
2 teaspoons cumin seeds
1 lemon, sliced very thinly
½ pint (300 ml) boiling stock or water
2 eggs, well beaten

———◆———

In a large shallow pan or wok, melt the butter and quickly fry the chicken. Remove the chicken to an ovenproof dish and place in a low oven at 300°F/150°C/gas 2. Fry the onion until brown in the same pan, then add to the chicken.

Excluding the stock and eggs, toss everything else in the wok or pan, adding a little more butter if it appears too dry. Add the stock or water and allow to bubble for about 3 minutes. Pour on to the chicken, and cook all together until heated through.

In a lightly oiled frying pan, cook the beaten egg gently until set. Be careful not to have the oil too hot – the egg is nicest when cooked enough to hold its shape but not to have hardened underneath. Cut the eggs into thin strips. Place these in a criss-cross pattern over the chicken and serve piping hot.

A THOUGHT ON HENS

I DO not make pets of fowls. . . . Still, quite apart from vulgar uses, it is pleasant to have a large establishment of dependants about you, looking to you for protection and maintenance. It imparts a certain patriarchal, Abrahamic magnificence to your conception of yourself.   EHA

Chicken with Prawn and Coconut Sauce

SERVES 6

An unusual combination of chicken and prawns, but one which works very well, especially with the coconut sauce.

6 chicken joints, halved and skinned
butter
1¼ lb (550 g) plain yoghurt
2–3 garlic cloves, crushed
½ teaspoon chilli powder
3 teaspoons ground cardamom
1 teaspoon ground turmeric
2 teaspoons ground coriander
4 oz (100 g) coconut cream, chopped
2 teaspoons cornflour
1 lb (450 g) cooked prawns
3 hard-boiled eggs, roughly chopped
chopped parsley

Place the pieces of chicken side by side in a shallow, buttered ovenproof dish. Mix together half the yoghurt, the garlic, chilli, cardamom, turmeric, coriander and chopped coconut (or melted if it has softened). Add to the chicken and cook in a hot oven at 400°F/200°C/gas 6 for 45 minutes. Test by piercing with a fork. Allow a little longer if the chicken juices run pink.

Meanwhile, in a saucepan heat the rest of the yoghurt with the cornflour. When it has thickened and boiled for about 3 minutes, add the prawns and the eggs.

Serve the chicken pieces and prawns side by side on the same plate with a small strip of chopped parsley between the two. The colour combination is very effective. The turmeric will have made the chicken a delightful yellow.

LAMB DISHES

The British love of lamb and mutton followed them to the subcontinent, although the heavy-fleeced sheep was not a natural creature of the tropics. In the mountains, sheep would have flourished, but elsewhere cooks would have had to rely on the occasional appearance in the market of 'mutton' (which was more normally goat or kid). In the nineteenth century, some British mutton lovers formed a club to rear a flock of sheep, and many individual families, if they had enough land, would rear a lamb or two. Lamb is also popular now with those who don't eat beef or pork (the Hindus and Moslems respectively).

Lamb is a wonderful meat for curries, as it marries very well with spices, absorbing them. As meat quality, casserole dishes and ovens vary so much, check if the meat is cooked after the recommended time – it should be soft and tender.

Badan Pasindah

SERVES 4

This dish could have been made with either mutton or goat. The Memsahib would have been delighted if her cook had managed to get lamb in the market. Badan Pasindah has such a marvellous aroma that it is one of the most welcoming dishes I know.

2 lb (900 g) boneless lamb, de-fatted and cut into ½ inch (1 cm) cubes
2–3 oz (50–75 g) butter or oil
1 lb (450 g) plain yoghurt

Coating mixture
1½ tablespoons ground coriander
1½ tablespoons paprika
2 teaspoons cornflour
½–2 teaspoons chilli powder
4 small or 2 large garlic cloves, crushed
5 tablespoons chopped fresh mint
a little salt

Coat the meat with the coating mixture, then fry in the butter or oil over a hot flame. Don't overcrowd your pan with meat as this disperses the heat too much, and the result is not as good. If you have a wok you will find it does the job better than a frying pan.

Any of the coating mixture left should be mixed with the yoghurt and poured over the meat in a heavy casserole. Cover and cook in a moderate oven at 350°F/180°C/gas 4 for about 1½ hours. Taste and test occasionally to ensure it doesn't overcook, and become dry. Add a little water if necessary.

Roghan Josh

SERVES 4

This is a well-known dish from Kashmir, and the name means red meat. It is wonderfully aromatic and rich, and does not need powerful chilli flavour for character – so if you want to leave the chilli powder out, why not?

3 fl oz (75 ml) ghee or oil
6 oz (175 g) onions, chopped
½ inch (1 cm) piece fresh ginger, peeled and chopped
8 cardamom pods, lightly crushed
1 teaspoon cumin seeds
6–8 garlic cloves, depending on size, chopped
1 teaspoon chilli powder
2 lb (900 g) leg or shoulder of lamb, de-fatted and cut into ½ inch (1 cm) cubes
2 teaspoons ground coriander
2 teaspoons ground turmeric
10 oz (275 g) plain yoghurt
8 oz (225 g) tomato passata (see page 17)
3 oz (75 g) coconut cream, chopped

Heat the ghee or oil in a deep, heavy casserole, and brown the onion. Add the ginger, cardmom, cumin, garlic and chilli. Tip in the meat and when you have coated it all well with the oil, add the coriander and turmeric. Follow this with the yoghurt, tomato and coconut. Mix well, cover and leave to cook in a moderately hot oven, at 375°F/190°C/gas 5, for about 1½ hours. Test occasionally.

You should have a lovely thick gravy – but when dealing with yoghurt, there is often a curdling which you may not like. The addition of a large tablespoon plain flour mixed with 4 tablespoons water will cure the problem. Cook into the finished dish for about 3–5 minutes.

THE CROW

I CAN call up no vision of Indian life without crows. Fancy refuses to conjure up the little bungalow at Dustypore in a happy state of crowlessness.

. . . The crow is a fungus of city life . . . I have never been able to discover any shred of grace about a crow . . .

It . . . dresses like a gentleman, carries itself jauntily . . . but . . . is a down-right . . . blackguard.   EHA

Koftas

◇

SERVES 4

 Koftas, or meatballs, are a speciality of central India. They can be made with beef as well. I once made them in one of those frantic situations that do – alas – crop up from time to time, with 1 lb of meat and ½ lb breadcrumbs. I can report that they were very nice.

◆

1½ lb (675 g) lean lamb, minced
1 egg
2½ oz (60 g) tomato purée
2 oz (50 g) onions, finely chopped
½ teaspoon chilli powder
2 teaspoons ground coriander
½ teaspoon cumin seeds or ground cumin
a little flour for coating
oil for deep- or shallow-frying

Sauce
1¼ lb (550 g) plain yoghurt
2 teaspoons cornflour
2 teaspoons turmeric
2 garlic cloves, crushed

◆

In a large bowl mix all the kofta ingredients. With clean, wet hands roll into small balls about 1 inch (2.5 cm) across. Roll these in flour. Deep-fry or shallow-fry as you like, until the meatballs have a firm crust (2–3 minutes should be enough, or 2 minutes each side if they have to be turned). Drain and put to one side.

To make the sauce, pour the yoghurt into a deep pan. Add the cornflour, turmeric and garlic, and mix thoroughly. Bring slowly to the boil, stirring from time to time to prevent sticking. When the sauce is plopping gently, add the meatballs, and simmer for 5–6 minutes before serving. A spinach dish and rice make good accompaniments.

Lamb with Coriander and Spinach

SERVES 6

Lamb and spinach is a combination that is popular all over India, and I have been given several versions of this dish. Needless to say they are all a little bit different. One of them uses the same amount of coriander and cardamom, but instead of using both spices completely ground they use half of each spice whole. This dish is lovely with rice and a dish of baked courgettes and tomato. The dish seems to improve with reheating, and it freezes beautifully.

4 fl oz (110 ml) cooking oil
10 cardamom pods, lightly bruised
2 teaspoons ground coriander
2 teaspoons coriander seeds
½ teaspoon ground cloves
1½ teaspoons chilli powder
2 garlic cloves, crushed
10 oz (275 g) onions, sliced
3 lb (1.4 kg) shoulder or leg of lamb, de-fatted and cut into ½ inch (1 cm) cubes
2 tablespoons plain flour
10 oz (275 g) plain yoghurt
1 lb (450 g) fresh spinach, washed and chopped
salt and freshly ground pepper

Get your oil very hot in a deep, heavy casserole, then add all the spices and the garlic. The coriander seeds will start popping quite alarmingly. Tip in the onions and allow to brown. Add the meat and seal all the pieces in the hot oil. Sprinkle the flour over the meat and mix well, then add the yoghurt. Cover and cook in a moderately hot oven at 375°F/190°C/gas 5 for 1½ hours. Taste to see if the meat is cooked, and cook a little longer if needed.

Cook the spinach in as little water as possible. Add to the casserole, mix in and adjust the seasoning. Serve immediately.

THE AYAH

THE *Ayah* is the "society" newspaper of small stations, and is indispensable. The barber is the general newsagent, and, as we part with our beards in the morning, we learn from him all particulars of the dinner at the general's last night, and of the engagement that resulted between the pretty Missy Baba and the captain. . . . But Old Tom is himself dependent on Ayahs, and there are matters beyond his range, matters which even in an Indian station cannot reach us by any male channel. They trickle from *madam* to *Ayah*, from *Ayah* to *Ayah*, and from *Ayah* to *madam*. Thus they ooze from house to house, and we are all saved from judging our neighbours by outward appearances. EHA

Lamb with Yoghurt and Ginger

SERVES 6

This dish is very good with rice and a dish of carrots cooked with butter and coriander seeds. Some chutney also makes a suitable accompaniment.

3 lb (1.4 kg) shoulder of lamb, de-fatted and cut into ½ inch (1 cm) cubes
3 fl oz (75 ml) cooking oil
3 oz (75 g) fresh ginger, peeled and finely chopped
3 garlic cloves, crushed
1 teaspoon chilli powder
9 cardamom pods, crushed, or 1 teaspoon ground cardamom
2 tablespoons plain flour
1 teaspoon ground turmeric
1¼ lb (550 g) plain yoghurt

Brown the lamb in the oil in a deep, heavy casserole. Add the ginger, garlic, chilli and cardamom. Sprinkle over the flour and turmeric, and mix well. Add the yoghurt, stir and cover. Cook in a moderately hot oven at 375°F/190°C/gas 5 for about 1½ hours.

Lamb with Cardamom and Coconut

SERVES 5

 I served this dish for Sunday brunch at my restaurant in Pewsey, Wiltshire, for many years. It was a great favourite with everyone and proved as popular there as it had been back in India.

2½ lb (1.1 kg) leg or shoulder of lamb, de-fatted and cut into ½ inch (1 cm) cubes
8 oz (225 g) onions, thinly sliced
4 tablespoons cooking oil
4 fresh or dried bay leaves, crumbled or sliced
2½ teaspoons ground cardamom
3 teaspoons ground cumin
1 teaspoon chilli powder
⅔ packet coconut cream (about 4½–5 oz/125–150 g), cut into pieces
salt and freshly ground pepper
1½ tablespoons plain flour (optional)

In a heavy casserole brown the meat and onions in the oil. Add the bay leaves, cardamom, cumin and chilli. Add the coconut pieces along with a little water. (The amount you add depends a lot on the size of casserole you are using, but as a rough guide I would suggest ½ pint/300 ml.) Cover and place in a moderately hot oven at 375°F/190°C/gas 5 for about 1½ hours.

When you feel it is just about ready, season if necessary. If you would like a thicker or smoother gravy dissolve the flour in 4 table-spoons water and add to the casserole. Cook for an extra 3 minutes.

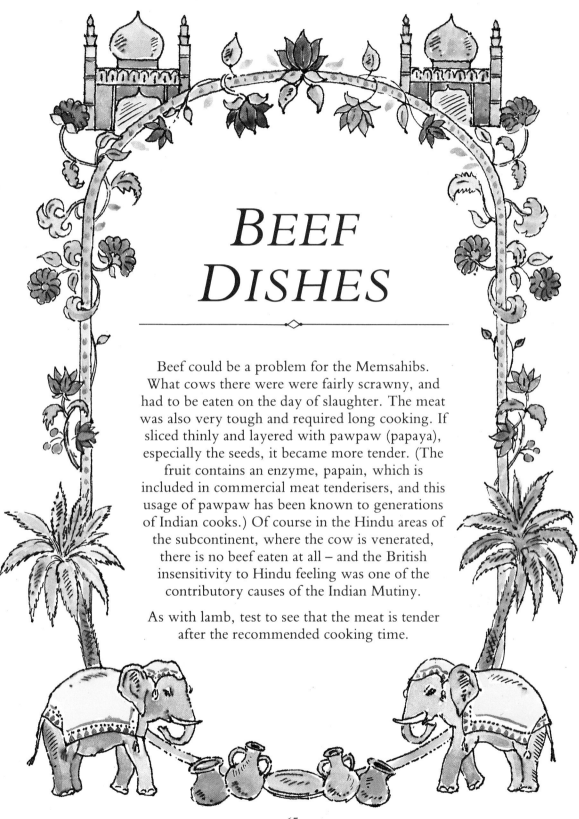

BEEF DISHES

Beef could be a problem for the Memsahibs. What cows there were were fairly scrawny, and had to be eaten on the day of slaughter. The meat was also very tough and required long cooking. If sliced thinly and layered with pawpaw (papaya), especially the seeds, it became more tender. (The fruit contains an enzyme, papain, which is included in commercial meat tenderisers, and this usage of pawpaw has been known to generations of Indian cooks.) Of course in the Hindu areas of the subcontinent, where the cow is venerated, there is no beef eaten at all – and the British insensitivity to Hindu feeling was one of the contributory causes of the Indian Mutiny.

As with lamb, test to see that the meat is tender after the recommended cooking time.

Charred Mince

SERVES 4

Minced beef dishes are very popular on the subcontinent. Authentic charred mince was scraped, not minced, and cooked in balls over hot coals or in the tandoori oven until well and truly charred. This, however, is an Anglicised version, and makes a very tasty dish.

◆

1½ lb (675 g) lean beef, minced
3½ oz (90 g) tomato purée
½ teaspoon chilli powder
juice of 1 lemon
3 tablespoons desiccated coconut
1½ teaspoons ground cumin

◆

Mix all the ingredients in a large bowl. Spread thinly in a greased tin, then slip under a very hot grill. When nice and black, turn over with a spatula, breaking up the lumps, and grill again. Continue until all is well cooked. Serve with rice and a sweet chutney.

TREE FROGS

TREE-frogs . . . flying themselves at a bed-post or a window-pane, and stick like a dab of mud, by virtue of those suckers on their toes.

One particular evening I was sitting in the garden, trying to finish a very interesting chapter in a book before it got too dark to read. . . . Within a few feet of me there was a projecting sunshade, and on it clung an enterprising tree-frog. To him my head loomed like some forest-clad mountain against the grey sky, and he guessed there might be game up there. So he wound up his leaping springs, took good aim, . . . and fired! I do not know exactly where he aimed, but he hit just behind my right ear, and, of course, *stuck*.

Now, I hold that half the art of telling a story . . . lies in knowing when to stop, so I will stop; suffice it to say, that since that evening I have admitted no exception to the general feeling of utter aversion with which I regard the whole race of frogs.   EHA

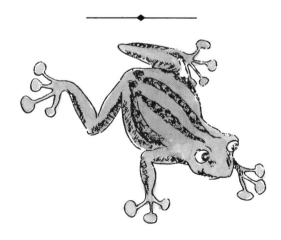

Quick-Fried Ginger Beef

SERVES 4

 This is a quick and simple dish from Ceylon, again using minced beef. It is nice served with rice, diced carrots, spinach and a side dish of fried banana slices.

2 onions, thinly sliced
3 tablespoons cooking oil
1½ lb (675 g) lean beef, minced
2 tablespoons grated fresh ginger
1 teaspoon ground cardamom
2 tablespoons chopped chutney
2 teaspoons ground coriander
salt and freshly ground pepper

Brown the onions in the oil, then remove from the pan. Fry the mince in the same pan until browned. Return the onions, and add all the other ingredients. Mix well, cook a little longer to heat through, and season if necessary.

Beef Kedgeree

SERVES 4

 The original Indian *khichri* was vegetarian, and it was the British who added fish to make a breakfast dish, and later meat for main-course dishes.

1 large onion, thinly sliced
2 fl oz (50 ml) cooking oil
1½ lb (675 g) lean beef, minced
1 teaspoon each of ground cumin, cardamom and turmeric
½ teaspoon chilli powder
6 oz (175 g) long-grain rice, cooked
1 small packet frozen peas, cooked
4 celery stalks, finely chopped
1 sweet red pepper, de-seeded and cut into little chunks

Fry the onion in the oil until brown. Mix the meat with the cumin, cardamom, turmeric and chilli and add to the onion, if you have a large enough frying pan. Otherwise remove the onions and then fry the meat. Add a little more oil if it seems necessary.

When the meat is well browned, add all the rest of the ingredients, and mix together. Make sure it is all nice and hot.

If you transfer the beef kedgeree to an ovenproof dish it will be quite happy in a moderate oven at 325°F/170°C/gas 3 until you are ready for it (for up to half an hour).

Lucknow Meatballs

SERVES 4

 Lucknow, the capital of Uttar Pradesh, is famous for its British Residency, besieged during the Indian Mutiny in 1857, and for its meatballs.

1½ lb (675 g) lean beef, minced
2 eggs
3½ oz (90 g) tomato purée
2 tablespoons desiccated coconut
2 teaspoons ground cardamom
1 teaspoon chilli powder
½ teaspoon ground cloves
½ teaspoon powdered cinnamon
a small amount of flour for coating
oil for frying

Sauce
2 tablespoons ground turmeric
2 tablespoons plain flour
1¼ lb (550 g) plain yoghurt

Mix all the meatball ingredients together and roll into small balls. Be firm to make sure they stick together. Roll in flour and either deep- or shallow-fry in oil. When all are brown on the outside, place in a shallow oven dish and cook for 10–15 minutes in a moderately hot oven at 375°F/190°C/gas 5.

Meanwhile make the sauce. Mix the turmeric, flour and 4 tablespoons of the yoghurt together. When smooth, add to the remainder of the yoghurt and heat in a large pan until thick and bubbling.

Tip the meatballs into the hot sauce and serve with rice and mango or lime chutney. This dish is given a party hat by a selection of side dishes – raisins, Bombay duck, chopped tomato, peanuts and crisply fried onions.

Beef with Tamarind and Yoghurt

SERVES 6

The tamarind and yoghurt here have a tenderising effect on the beef. The tamarind also brings out the other flavours in the same way that lemon juice does.

◆

3 tablespoons ground coriander
2 teaspoons ground cumin
1–2 teaspoons chilli powder
2 oz (50 g) plain flour
2½ lb (1.1 kg) topside of beef, cut into ½ inch (1 cm) cubes
4 fl oz (110 ml) oil or ghee
6 oz (175 g) block tamarind, broken into pieces, or 4 oz (100 g)
tamarind pulp, both soaked in ½ pint (300 ml) boiling water
1¼ lb (550 g) plain yoghurt
3 oz (75 g) coconut cream, cut into pieces

◆

Mix together the coriander, cumin, chilli and flour. Coat the chunks of meat in the spice mixture and fry in the oil. Do just a few pieces at a time or the oil loses too much heat and doesn't brown the meat properly.

Push the soaked block tamarind through a sieve into a bowl. Add the tamarind liquid, yoghurt and coconut to the meat. Mix well. Pour into a heavy casserole with a well fitting lid and cook in a moderately hot oven at 375°F/190°C/gas 5 for roughly 1½ hours. Try a bit at this stage, and then act accordingly. If it has been bubbling very vigorously, it may need a little more water.

THE BOY

The House-boy

YOUR boy is your *valet de chambre*, your butler, your tailor, your steward and general agent, your interpreter, or oriental translator and your treasurer. On assuming charge of his duties he takes steps first, in an unobtrusive way, to ascertain the amount of your income, both that he may know the measure of his dignity, and also that he may be able to form an estimate of what you ought to spend. This is a matter with which he feels he is officially concerned. Indeed, the arrangement which accords best with his own view of his position and responsibilities is that, as you draw your salary each month, you should make it over to him in full. . . . If you have not a large enough soul to consent to this arrangement, he is not discouraged. . . . At the end of the month he presents you a faithful account of his expenditure, the purport of which is plainly this, that since you did not hand over your salary to him at the beginning of the month, you are to do so now. . . .   EHA

Beef with
Bay Leaves and Fresh Ginger

SERVES 4

Beef and ginger go well together. I sometimes use a packet of tomato passata (see page 17) made up to 1 pint (600 ml) with water instead of the plain water, just for a change.

½ teaspoon each of chilli powder, ground cloves and powdered cinnamon
1 teaspoon ground turmeric
2 teaspoons ground cumin
3 teaspoons fresh chopped ginger
2 fl oz (50 ml) (at least) cooking oil or ghee
2 lb (900 g) stewing beef, de-fatted and cut into ½ inch (1 cm) cubes
4 fresh bay leaves, thinly sliced, or dried, crumbled
½ packet coconut cream (about 3½ oz/90 g), cut into small pieces
1 pint (600 ml) water
1 tablespoon flour (optional)

Pour all the spices into the oil in a heavy casserole and fry for 1 minute. Add the beef and bay leaves. Have the heat high. Turn the pieces of beef over so that they are all well covered in both the oil and the spices. Add the coconut and the water.

Cover and cook in a moderately hot oven at 375°F/190°C/gas 5 for 1½ hours. A tablespoon of flour mixed with 4 tablespoons water added to the casserole will thicken it if too thin (cook for a few moments longer).

Beef Bandaloo

SERVES 6

I was lucky enough to meet a delightful old lady called Cecile Grant, who had a scrapbook of Anglo-Indian recipes, some handwritten, some cut from local newspapers and yellowed with age. This was one of them, and I quote it exactly. For reference, 1 *chatak* (or *chittack*) is 2 oz (50 g), 1 *seer* is 2 lb (900 g).

1½ *seers* beef cut into ½ inch cubes marinated in 1 teacup vinegar

Spice mix
8 red chillies
2 tablespoons *dhania* (coriander)
2 tablespoons mustard seed
4 pieces *huldi* (turmeric)
½ *chatak jeera* (cumin)
1 *chatak* ginger (fresh)

Grind all the spice mix ingredients and fry in
3 *chataks* gee
2 *chataks* mustard oil

Add the meat and vinegar and simmer until the meat is soft.

It is correct for red oil to float to the top of this dish.

Serve with chapatis to dip into the flavourful oil.

PORK DISHES

Pork is not widely eaten in India, as the pig is considered unclean by the Moslems. It is, however, a speciality of Goa, a coastal region to the south-west, once a Portuguese colony, and where the inhabitants are mainly Christian Indian as a result. Pigs are not seen much in India, except in Goa and in the very north of the subcontinent. The Sahibs attempted to breed pigs, enjoying some success in the mountains, and they would have eaten the wild boar they hunted for sport. It would undoubtedly have caused the Memsahibs some anxiety, working out which member of her kitchen staff could be called upon to cook the bacon for breakfast.

Pork with Bay Leaves and Coconut

SERVES 6

 The Indian bay leaf is the aromatic leaf of the evergreen cassia tree (the same tree which provides cassia bark, an alternative to cinnamon), and it has quite a different flavour from our laurel bay leaf. Pork marries wonderfully with the flavours of cardamom and coconut.

2½ lb (1.1 kg) sparerib of pork, de-fatted and cut into ½ inch (1 cm) cubes
3 tablespoons plain flour
2 teaspoons coriander seeds
1 teaspoon ground cardamom
1 teaspoon chilli powder (vary to taste)
2 bay leaves, crumbled if dry, sliced if fresh
4 fl oz (110 ml) ghee or oil
4 oz (100 g) coconut cream, broken into pieces
1 pint (600 ml) water
salt and freshly ground pepper

Toss the meat in the flour. Fry the dry spices and bay leaves in the oil in a deep casserole over a high heat. When the coriander seeds start popping, add the meat and brown. When very brown add the coconut and water. Mix well, and season to taste. Cover and cook in a moderately hot oven at 375°F/190°C/gas 5 for about 1½ hours until tender. Test for readiness after an hour.

Pork with Peanuts

SERVES 6

Cashews may be used instead of peanuts in this recipe. In the original recipes, the peanuts would have been pulverised to powder and oil in the pestle and mortar (long a major utensil in the Indian kitchen, and essential for each cook to grind his own special mixture of masala or curry powder). Using peanut butter makes the whole process very much easier.

---

2 onions, thinly sliced
4 fl oz (110 ml) oil or ghee
2½ lb (1.1 kg) sparerib pork, de-fatted and cut into ½ inch (1 cm) cubes
4 large tablespoons peanut butter
4 teaspoons ground cumin
½ teaspoon powdered cinnamon
1 teaspoon chilli powder (alter to taste)
2 teaspoons soft brown sugar
2 oz (50 g) plain flour
1 pint (600 ml) water
salt and freshly ground pepper

Fry the onions in the oil in a large casserole until brown, and then remove. Brown the pork in batches in the oil, then add the onions, peanut butter, spices, sugar and flour. Mix well, add the water, and season to taste. Cook in a moderately hot oven at 375°F/190°C/gas 5 for about 1½ hours, tasting after 1 hour.

SNAKES

POISONOUS snakes are a great mystery. Out of a class of animals so harmless, so gentle, and so gracefully beautiful, one here and one there, for no assignable reason, carries with it an instrument exquisitely contrived for inflicting almost instant death on creatures fifty times its own size . . . thus . . . blasting the reputation of the whole family, and making us shun and abhor a race which would be universal favourites, not only on account of their grace and the brightness of their hues, but for their intelligence and the pleasantness of their dispositions. EHA

Tandoori Pork

—————◇—————

SERVES 4

The tandoor, a cylindrical, charcoal-fired clay oven, was developed in north-west India, now Pakistan, and spread only in the last 50 years to elsewhere on the subcontinent. As a result only the earlier Memsahibs posted in north-west India would have been aware of the technique, although post-war cooks would possibly have encountered it, as in this grill adaptation. The essence of tandoori meat cooking is marinating then a speedy cooking at a very high heat.

————◆————

2 lb (900 g) pork tenderloin, cut into ½ inch (1 cm) thick slices
oil

Marinade
1¼ lb (550 g) plain yoghurt
3 teaspoons ground turmeric
½ teaspoon chilli powder
2 teaspoons ground coriander
1½ teaspoons ground cumin
½ teaspoon ground allspice
2 tablespoons tomato purée (optional)

————◆————

Mix the marinade ingredients together and immerse the pork slices in it for at least 1 hour (overnight, chilled, is better).

Oil a shallow ovenproof dish or tin, and spread the meat pieces over it. Brown under a medium grill, then turn the pieces over and grill until brown on the other side. Serve immediately.

The tomato purée gives the traditional red colour to the tandoori meat, but it may be omitted.

Pork Vindaloo

SERVES 6

 Vindaloo means 'hot' to most people, and this dish, traditionally made with pork, comes from Goa and South India. Vindaloos were very popular with the Sahibs, the hotter the better, and they would pile their plates over-indulgently high – and sleep it off in the afternoons! When Soloman, our cook in Ceylon, was on leave, Apuhamie, his assistant, would cook for us. The first curry was so hot, we just sat there, tears streaming down our faces, unable even to speak. The only one unaffected was James, aged three. It seemed he had been eating similar curries in the kitchen for months!

◆

2 tablespoons plain flour
1 tablespoon ground coriander
3 teaspoons ground cumin
1–2 teaspoons chilli powder
1 teaspoon ground turmeric
2½ lb (1.1 kg) sparerib pork, de-fatted and cut into ½ inch (1 cm) cubes
4 fl oz (110 ml) oil or ghee
2 bay leaves, crumbled if dry, thinly sliced if fresh
2 garlic cloves, chopped
4 oz (100 g) tomato passata (see page 17)
1 pint (600 ml) water
2 tablespoons lemon juice
salt and freshly ground pepper

◆

Mix the flour with all the spices, then toss the pork in it. Fry the meat and spicy flour until brown in the oil or ghee. Add the bay leaves, garlic, tomato, water and lemon juice and season to taste.

Either simmer on the top of the stove or cook in a moderately hot oven at 375°F/190°C/gas 5 for about 1½ hours. Taste after an hour.

Burma Pork

❖

SERVES 6

Pork is the favourite meat of Burma and other countries of the East – China, for instance – and this combination of pork and prawns, taken from a 1930 s cookbook, has a delicious flavour.

◆

6 tablespoons oil
2 onions, sliced
2 inch (5 cm) piece fresh ginger, peeled and thinly sliced
3–4 garlic cloves, chopped
4 tomatoes, quartered
2 lb (900 g) sparerib of pork, de-fatted and cut into ½ inch (1 cm) cubes
3 oz (75 g) coconut cream, broken into pieces
soy sauce (not necessary, but very nice)
salt
8 oz (225 g) prawns, shelled

◆

Pour the oil into a casserole and heat. When very hot, add the onion, ginger, garlic and tomato. Add the meat and coconut, plus a little water if it seems too dry. Cover and cook either on the stove or in a moderately hot oven at 375°F/190°C/gas 5 for roughly an hour – but test after 45 minutes.

Add the soy sauce and/or salt if they are needed, along with the prawns. Heat through for a few minutes, then serve immediately.

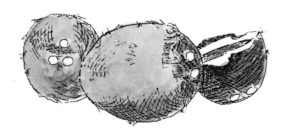

THE BODYGUARD

HE is like a carriage clock, able to sleep in any conceivable position; and such is his mental constitution that, when not sleeping, he is able to "be present" hour after hour without feeling any desire for change of occupation. *Ennui* never troubles him, time never hangs heavy on his hands; he sits as patiently as a cow and chews the cud of *pan suparee*, and he bespatters the walls with a sanguinary pigment produced by the mastication of the same. He needs no food, but he goes out to drink water thirty-five times a day, and, when he returns refreshed, a certain acrid odour penetrates every crevice of the house, almost dislodging the rats and exterminating the lesser vermin. To liken it to the smell of tobacco would give civilized mankind a claim against me for defamation of character.   EHA

Pork Fillet with Dhal and Coriander

SERVES 4–6

Dhal dishes – usually lentil – are served by themselves, with vegetables, or with meat, and are very popular. This recipe is from a post-war cookbook.

8 oz (225 g) dhal (lentils), soaked for at least 2 hours (best overnight)
in 1 pint (600 ml) water
1 pint (600 ml) water
2 garlic cloves, crushed
½ teaspoon chilli powder
a little salt
2 tablespoons freshly ground (if possible) coriander
½ teaspoon finely chopped fresh ginger
2 onions, sliced
4 or 6 tablespoons oil or ghee
2 pork fillets, trimmed and cut into ½ inch (1 cm) slices
about 1½ tablespoons plain flour, if necessary

Drain the dhal and place in a large pan with the fresh water, the garlic, chilli, a little salt, the coriander and ginger. Simmer for about 30 minutes, stirring occasionally to prevent sticking.

Fry the onion in half the oil until brown. Add to the dhal. Fry the pieces of pork in batches in the rest of the oil. As the meat is cooked add it to the dhal. Adjust the seasoning and serve.

If the dhal separates or appears too runny, add a little flour dissolved in 4–5 tablespoons of water, and cook for a few more minutes.

RICE AND SIDE DISHES

Most of the rice of India is grown in Bengal and there are 20 to 30 different types, the two most commonly mentioned in old cookbooks being basmati and patna. Elsewhere, wheat was the staple crop and bread, not rice, was the basic accompaniment to curries.

Vegetables and salads in the days of the Mem-sahibs were submerged in water for up to an hour with crystals of potash (a very strong disinfectant) to kill any germs. This resulted in a loss of texture, and a disgusting taste. The unhealthy nature of the vegetables was thought to be caused by watering during growth with dirty water.

Fresh side dishes were popular; little tasty morsels – usually the only raw ingredients in the Mem-sahib's repertoire – to sprinkle on or serve with curries.

Yellow Rice

SERVES 6–8

 If you can manage it, fresh coconut milk will enhance the dish considerably. If, however, you don't have any, pour 1½ pints (900 ml) boiling water over 8 oz (225 g) desiccated coconut. Allow to rest for 15 minutes and then squeeze out the liquid. Don't throw the reconstituted coconut away. Keep for a dish of Sine Sambol (see page 94).

1 lb (450 g) long-grain rice
1½ pints (900 ml) coconut milk
1 teaspoon ground cumin
2 teaspoons ground turmeric
a little salt

Bring all the ingredients to the boil and then simmer for as long as the rice packet demands.

If the rice seems cooked but is still quite wet, pour into a shallow dish and dry out in a moderate over at 350°F/180°C/gas 4 for roughly 20 minutes. Cover it lightly and toss the grains over from time to time with a fork to prevent the top layer of rice from hardening.

Otherwise simply loosen the grains with a fork. Put the lid tightly on and leave the rice to keep warm until needed. It will keep its heat for about half an hour, and the steam will ensure the grains are fluffy and separate, which is how Indian rice is always served.

PEELAJEE, THE MALEE

HERE, in India, we have need of Peelajee. He is a necessary part of the machinery by which our exile life is made to be the graceful thing it often is. I pass by bungalow after bungalow, each in its own little paradise, and look upon the green lawn successfully defying an unkind climate, the islands of mingled foliage in profuse, confused beauty, the gay flower beds, the clean gravel paths with their trim borders, the grotto in a shady corner, where fern and moss mingle, all dripping as if from recent showers and make you feel cool in spite of all thermometers, and I say to myself, "Without the *Malee* all this would not be." . . . keeping a *Malee* draws you out, for he compels you to look after him, and if you are to look after him, you must know something about his art, and if you do not know, you must learn. So we Anglo-Indians are gardeners almost to a man, and spend many pure, happy hours with the pruning shears and the budding knife, and this we owe to the *Malee*.

. . . He is a fatalist in philosophy, and this helps him too. For example, when he transplants a rose bush, he saves himself the trouble of digging very deep by breaking the root, for if the plant is to live it will live, and if it is to die it will die. Some plants live, he remarks, and some plants die. The second half of this aphorism is only too true. In fact, many of my best plants not only die, but suddenly and entirely disappear.   EHA

Pullao Rice

SERVES 4–6

This rather basic recipe was taken from a handwritten cookbook.

---

12 oz (350 g) Basmati rice, washed
1½ pints (900 ml) water
2 tablespoons sunflower oil
1 tablespoon desiccated coconut
8 cardamom pods, crushed

Toss all the ingredients into the boiling water, and boil slowly for about 10 minutes without a lid. Fluff up with a fork and taste; if more cooking is needed, cook for another 5 minutes or so. Fluff up again and cover; turn off the heat and leave to dry out completely.

Should the rice still be very wet, strain off the extra water and dry in a moderate oven as for Yellow Rice on page 85.

Lentils and Rice

SERVES 6–8

 This is an approximation of the original *khichri* which later became the Anglo-Indian kedgeree. It is lovely with meat, chicken or fish.

8 oz (225 g) lentils
water
8 oz (225 g) long-grain rice
a little salt
½ teaspoon ground turmeric
1 teaspoon ground cardamom
2 fl oz (50 ml) oil

Soak the lentils in 1 pint (600 ml) water for an hour or so, then cook in fresh water to cover until soft but not mushy, about 20 minutes. Drain if necessary.

Boil the rice in 1 pint (600 ml) lightly salted water for about 10–12 minutes until cooked. Drain off any excess water.

Fry the turmeric and cardomom in the oil for a minute or so, then fold, with the rice, into the lentils. Place in a shallow dish, lightly cover and dry and finish cooking in a moderate oven at 350°F/180°C/gas 4 for about 10–15 minutes.

Sour Beans

SERVES 4

Meat curries tend to be cooked slowly over a long period. Quite the opposite happens with vegetable dishes, which are cooked as quickly as possible. The Memsahib may have been a bit alarmed when she first came across *brinjal* and okra, but all her old favourites such as cauliflower, tomato, spinach and cabbage were there, as well as the ubiquitous bean. This recipe comes from a private Ceylon cookbook.

◆

1 lb (450 g) green beans, sliced
2 tablespoons ghee or butter
1 onion, finely chopped
2 garlic cloves, crushed
2 teaspoons ground coriander
2 tablespoons tamarind juice
300 ml (½ pint) coconut milk (see page 16)

◆

Blanch the beans for 3 minutes in boiling water and then drain. Melt the ghee or butter in a deep pan and fry the onion until brown. Add the garlic and coriander, and fry for 1 minute. Add the beans and mix well. In a separate bowl mix the tamarind juice and the coconut milk together and pour over the beans. Simmer for 5 minutes and serve.

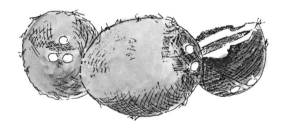

Cauliflower Foogath

SERVES 4

 I have made this dish with potato, and found it very interesting. Fresh ginger has a lovely flavour which is quite different from dried, and it seems to complement vegetable dishes. If you search, you might be able to get hold of fresh turmeric – known as Indian saffron, and a rhizome rather like ginger. It has a lovely flavour, and is especially nice served chopped and raw in salads.

1½ lb (675 g) cauliflower
4 tablespoons cooking oil or ghee
8 oz (225 g) onion, chopped
1½ inches (4 cm) fresh root ginger, peeled and very finely chopped
1 teaspoon ground turmeric, or 3–4 teaspoons chopped fresh turmeric
(see above)
6 fl oz (175 ml) coconut milk (see page 16)

Separate the cauliflower into sprigs and chop any excess stalk into small pieces. Heat the oil in a large saucepan and fry the onion until brown. Add the ginger and turmeric, followed by the cauliflower. Mix well and then pour in the coconut milk. Cover and simmer for 6–7 minutes, then remove the lid and give it a good stir. Continue cooking for a further 3–4 minutes – the cauliflower should be still a little crisp.

EARLY MORNING

WHEN the sun has just risen, and the cold, delicious morning air waves the scented grass, with the frozen beetles clinging to it, and the birds sing, and you hear them sing, because there is no Babel of worldly noises and vile clangour of coarse-minded crows to drown their music . . .

At such times to ramble aimlessly along, and simply drink in the enjoyment which seems to be poured out of the face of Nature, makes a man feel that his capacity for pure animal happiness is too limited.   EHA

Bengal Brinjal

SERVES 4

 Many Indians are vegetarians, but not many Memsahibs were. These lovely vegetarian dishes were used, therefore, as side dishes with meat, much as we use them today. Although fresh chilli gives this dish a lovely flavour, it was seldom added on the Memsahib's table. This dish is especially nice with lamb.

---

2 fl oz (50 ml) cooking oil or ghee
8 oz (225 g) onion, sliced
2 teaspoons coriander seeds
1 teaspoon cumin seeds
2 bay leaves, sliced
½ teaspoon chopped fresh chilli (optional)
2 garlic cloves, crushed
1½ lb (675 g) aubergine, sliced
300 ml (½ pint) water or stock
4 tablespoons tomato ketchup
salt and freshly ground pepper if necessary

Heat the oil in a deep pan, add the onion, and fry until a golden brown. Add the seeds, bay leaves, chilli and garlic. When the seeds start popping (they do so in a most aggressive manner), add the aubergine. Turn once or twice to make sure all the slices are lightly cooked. Mix the water or stock with the ketchup and pour over the aubergine. Simmer over a low heat with the lid on the pan for about 10 minutes. Stir once or twice during the process. If it should get too dry, add a little more liquid.

The ketchup should supply a salty enough flavour, but do taste and add seasoning to suit yourself.

Spiced Pumpkin or Green Pawpaw

SERVES 4

 Unripe pawpaw would have been used quite a lot as a vegetable when pumpkin, swedes or potatoes were not available. Sweet potatoes and yams never quite caught the imagination of the Memsahibs, and even in my day, they were not popular with very many wives. This recipe is from Ceylon.

1½ lb (675 g) pumpkin or green pawpaw, peeled, deseeded and cut into
½ inch (1 cm) chunks
3 oz (75 g) ghee or butter
1 large eating apple, peeled, cored and sliced
1 large red onion, about 6 oz (175 g), sliced
2 teaspoons sugar
½ teaspoon powdered cinnamon
1 teaspoon ground cardamom
300 ml (½ pint) coconut milk (see page 16)

Lightly fry the pumpkin or pawpaw in the ghee, then remove to a shallow casserole. Fry the apple and onion in the remaining ghee until the onion is golden brown. Add the sugar, cinnamon and cardamom. Pour the coconut milk over the pumpkin, and cook in a medium oven pre-heated to 375°F/190°C/gas 5 for 35–45 minutes.

Sine Sambol

This dish was very popular in Ceylon, and was served with almost all curries.

Pour enough boiling water over 5 tablespoons desiccated coconut to just cover it. Leave for 20 minutes. Squeeze the coconut until it is dry and fluff it up. (Keep the coconut milk separate to use in curries or in the tomato and onion dish following.) Mix the coconut with at least 3 teaspoons chilli powder and 3 teaspoons fresh lime juice (lemon is not nearly as nice). This is very hot and you only sprinkle a little over your curry, but it has a lovely flavour.

Quick Side Dishes

Onion, Tomato and Coconut

Using the coconut milk left over from the Sine Sambol above, add as much very thinly sliced onion and tomato as it will comfortably hold.

Raita

Grate about 7 inches (18 cm) peeled cucumber. Squeeze dry, and discard the liquid. Squeeze plenty of garlic into the cucumber, 4 medium cloves at least. Add 5 oz (150 g) plain yoghurt and mix well.

Red Pepper and Cucumber

Roast a sweet red pepper over the gas flame or under the grill and then rub off the scorched skin. Halve and de-seed, then chop into little pieces. Mix with an equal amount of grated, squeezed cucumber.

Aubergine and Sesame Seeds with Lime

Slice 6 oz (175 g) aubergines very thinly. Simmer in 6 fl oz (175 ml) water until soft. Add 2 teaspoons lime juice and 2 teaspoons sesame seeds, and mix well together.

Spinach and Coriander Seeds

Cook 8 oz (225 g) washed and finely chopped spinach in a little butter with, if possible, no extra water. While it is cooking, add 2 teaspoons coriander seeds that have been briefly tossed in sizzling butter.

Carrot and Coriander Seeds

Grate carrots and mix with coriander seeds that have been briefly fried in some oil.

Fried Bananas/Onions

Fry thinly sliced bananas or onions in oil until brown, then drain and leave to go cold.

Yoghurt, Anchovy and Egg

Mix chopped anchovies and hard-boiled eggs into plain yoghurt.

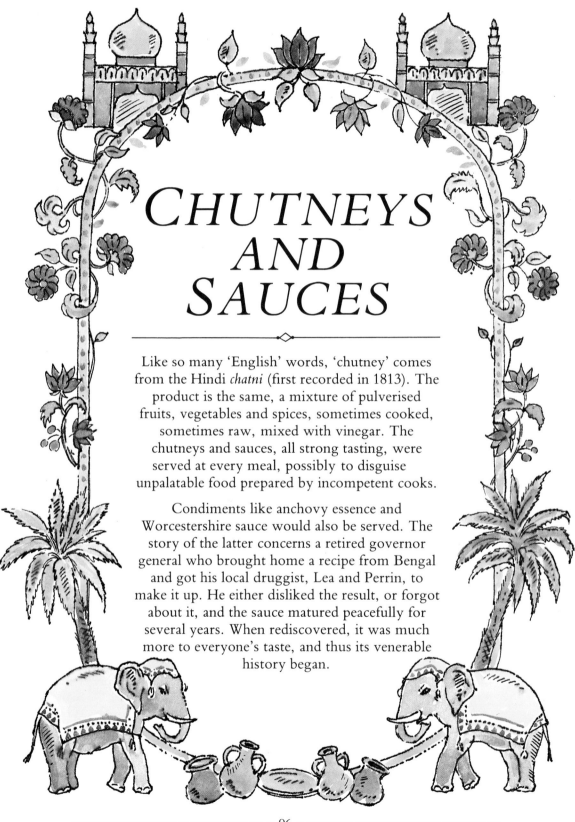

CHUTNEYS AND SAUCES

Like so many 'English' words, 'chutney' comes from the Hindi *chatni* (first recorded in 1813). The product is the same, a mixture of pulverised fruits, vegetables and spices, sometimes cooked, sometimes raw, mixed with vinegar. The chutneys and sauces, all strong tasting, were served at every meal, possibly to disguise unpalatable food prepared by incompetent cooks.

Condiments like anchovy essence and Worcestershire sauce would also be served. The story of the latter concerns a retired governor general who brought home a recipe from Bengal and got his local druggist, Lea and Perrin, to make it up. He either disliked the result, or forgot about it, and the sauce matured peacefully for several years. When rediscovered, it was much more to everyone's taste, and thus its venerable history began.

Wentworth Chutney

MAKES ABOUT 4½ lb (2 kg)

An apple, raisin and date chutney, from a printed cookbook of 1913. I'm afraid that the origin of the name wasn't passed down to me.

◆

2 lb (900 g) cooking apples, peeled, cored and chopped
1 lb (450 g) raisins
1 lb (450 g) dates, stoned and chopped
2 oz (50 g) fresh ginger, peeled and finely chopped
2–3 garlic cloves, peeled and crushed
½ teaspoon powdered cinnamon
white or brown vinegar
8 oz (225 g) soft brown sugar

◆

Put the apples, raisins, dates and ginger in a pan with the garlic and cinnamon. Pour over enough vinegar to barely cover the fruits, and simmer very gently until the apples are completely soft. Add the sugar and simmer for 20 minutes.

At this stage it should be just right for pouring into jam-jars. However, apples vary, and if the chutney seems to be too runny turn up the heat and give it a 10-minute hard boil to evaporate some of the excess liquid.

Put non-corrosive lids on the jars when they are cold.

Bengal Chutney

All three of these recipes come from private cookbooks. All the fruits, vegetables and spices are conveniently minced or processed together. (Try it both ways as you get two very different textures.) Add the vinegar right at the end, using more or less than that recommended in the recipe, according to how thick you like your chutney.

Best of all, there is no cooking involved!

Bottle in clean jars with non-corrosive tops, and keep for at least two weeks before using. Once opened, keep your chutney in the cold larder or the refrigerator.

◆

I *Makes about 7 lb (3.2 kg)*
2 lb (900 g) plums, stoned
12 oz (350 g) fresh ginger, peeled
1 lb (450 g) unripe mangoes, peeled and stoned
2 oz (50 g) garlic, skinned
1 lb (450 g) tamarind pulp
4 oz (100 g) chillies, de-seeded
1 lb (450 g) soft brown sugar
1 tablespoon salt
1 lb (450 g) onions, peeled and quartered
1 pint (600 ml) white or brown vinegar

◆

II *Makes about 11 lb (5 kg)*
4 lb (1.8 kg) plums, stoned
1 lb (450 g) dates, stoned
1½ lb (675 g) unripe mangoes, peeled and stoned
4 oz (100 g) garlic, skinned
8 oz (225 g) tamarind pulp
4 oz (100 g) chillies, de-seeded
1½ lb (675 g) soft brown sugar
2 teaspoons salt
2 lb (900 g) onions, peeled and quartered
6 cardamom seeds (not pods)
1 teaspoon powdered cinnamon
1 pint (600 ml) white or brown vinegar

III   *Makes about 6½ lb (3 kg)*
1½ lb (675 g) plums, stoned
12 oz (350 g) fresh ginger, peeled
4 oz (100 g) dates, stoned
12 oz (350 g) green tomatoes, halved
2 oz (50 g) garlic, skinned
1 lb (450 g) tamarind pulp
2 oz (50 g) chillies, de-seeded
1 lb (450 g) brown sugar
1 teaspoon salt
1 lb (450 g) onions, peeled and quartered
¾ pint (450 ml) white or brown vinegar

Sherry Peppers

 This was something every household had, and there were many variations. Each household was extremely proud of its own special mixture and swore it was vastly superior to everyone else's.

A good basic brew is very simple. You need a clean jam-jar with a non-corrosive lid. Fill it loosely with those tiny little chilli peppers (red or green) that have so much flavour, not to mention considerable fire-power. Big chillies can be used sliced, but are not as good on either count. Top up your jar with sherry (or whisky, which we prefer) and put the lid on very firmly. Leave this tasty fire-water in your store-cupboard for about three months and then permit yourself two or three drops in your bowl of soup or casserole. The flavour grows with time.

For variations, add a cardamom pod or two, a piece of fresh ginger, or a few cumin seeds.

A little warning – a few drops **means** just exactly that!!

THE BUTLER (*continued*)

. . . HAVE you ever stepped back a few paces and contemplated, not your own or anyone else's individual servant, but the entire phenomenon of an Indian Butler? Here is a man whose food by nature is curry and rice, before a hillock of which he sits cross-legged, and putting his five fingers into it, makes a large bolus, which he pushes into his mouth. He repeats this till all is gone, and then he sleeps like a boa-constrictor until he recovers his activity; or else he feeds on great flat cakes of wheat flour, off which he rends jagged pieces and lubricates them with some spicy and unctuous gravy. All our ways of life, our meats and drinks, and all our notions of propriety and fitness in connection with the complicated business of appeasing our hunger as becomes our station, all these are a foreign land to him: yet he has made himself altogether at home in them.   EHA

Bridget Aitken's Guava Jelly

MAKES ABOUT 5 lb (2.25 kg)

This recipe comes from my mother-in-law's cookbook, and probably dates from the 1920s. It is quite one of the richest, most luxurious jellies, wonderful with hare, rabbit, venison and lamb and, best of all, hot buttered toast!

The only British equivalent to the guava – although these can now be bought in ethnic shops and more enlightened supermarkets – is the old-fashioned medlar. You can only get medlars in October and you don't make your jelly until they are squashy and over-ripe, not a pretty sight.

5 lb (2.25 kg) guavas
2 large or 3 small limes
sugar

Quarter the guavas and the limes and place them in a large preserving pan with just enough water to cover them. Simmer the fruit until completely soft, crushing it from time to time.

Strain through a jelly-bag overnight. The next day measure out 1 lb (450 g) sugar for every pint (600 ml) liquid.

Return the liquid and sugar to the preserving pan and cook gently until the sugar has dissolved, and then boil rapidly until you have a good 'set'. Dribble a little on to a clean cold saucer to test – if it wrinkles when pushed with a finger, it's ready.

Brinjal Pickle

MAKES ABOUT 8½ lb (3.75 kg)

 An aubergine pickle from a 1930s recipe. To remind you, 1 *seer* is 2 lb (900 g), 1 *chatak* 2 oz (50 g).

2 *seers brinjal* [aubergine], cut into ½ inch (1 cm) cubes
½ *seer* fresh ginger
¼ *seer* garlic, crushed
1 *chatak* mustard seed
1 *chatak huldi* [turmeric]
½ *chatak jeera* [cumin]
½ *chatak* fresh green chillies
½ *chatak* dried red chillies
1 dessertspoon *mathee* [fenugreek] seeds
1 tablespoon salt
1 *seer* oil
1 pint vinegar
¼ *seer* dark brown sugar

Simmer everything for about 30 minutes, and bottle when all is soft and integrated.

The Sahib's Sauce

MAKES ABOUT 1½ lb (700 g)

This sauce is *not* for the faint-hearted! It has a long shelf-life when bottled, and makes a most exotic and unusual present. It comes from a scrapbook of recipes of the turn of the century.

◆

20 hot peppers, red or green, roughly 4 inches (10 cm) long
1 lb (450 g) marrow or unripe pawpaws
4 large onions, chopped
4 tablespoons olive oil
6 garlic cloves, crushed
10 oz (275 g) Dijon mustard
1 heaped teaspoon ground turmeric

◆

Cut the peppers into little rings, keeping the seeds. Cut the marrow into small chunks, keeping the seeds only if the vegetable is young. If you use pawpaw, cut it into chunks but discard the seeds.

In a big, heavy-based pan, fry the onion in the oil. When faintly coloured, add the peppers and the marrow. Brown for 2–3 minutes, then add all the other ingredients. Turn down the heat and simmer, stirring frequently, until the mixture is soft and well cooked. Mash to a purée and bottle.

THE HEAVENLY SHREW

"THE unfortunate nobleman who now languishes in Dartmoor jail" has not been more ill-used and misrepresented than this poor creature. It is not a rat at all, neither *Mus* this nor *Mus* that, but *Sorex cœrulescens*, which means the heavenly shrew. And, if it is not a rat in name, it is still less that villainous thing in nature. It wants none of your provisions, and wanton destruction is not in all its thoughts; its sole purpose in the house is a friendly one, *videlicet*, to hunt the loathsome cockroach and the

pestiferous beetle. It is charged with diffusing an unpleasant odour, and there is undoubtedly some truth in this; it can be very unsavoury at times. But that is not its normal state; it is the fruit of vexation of spirit. An unpersecuted musk-rat is most inoffensive. In short, that quality which brings the meek little animal into such bad odour, so to speak, is the defensive armour with which Nature has provided it, and every time you hunt a musk-rat you justify the provision. Lastly, one small fault may well be overlooked in view of the many amiable virtues that adorn its character. While the rat, after a night of crime, spends the day in a sanguinary *fracas* with its own brothers in the ceiling, . . . the days of the heavenly shrew are passed in sweet domestic harmony. As night comes on, the pair venture out of their hole and meander along together, warbling to one another in gentle undertones. Or perhaps the little ones at home are growing up, and their mamma brings them out to see the world. The first-born takes hold of her tail in its teeth, its tail is grasped by the next, and so on to the little Benjamin at the end, and thus the whole family, like a hairy serpent, wriggles away together – a sight, I admit, to make one's flesh creep; but, looked at in a proper spirit, it is a moving spectacle, full of moral beauty.

———————◆———————

Devil's Paste

 This evil little mixture – not dissimilar to the Patum Peperium (or Gentleman's Relish) invented in 1828 – can become quite addictive! Spread it on steaks and chops before you grill them; make little slits in fillets of fish or chicken breasts and fill with the paste; and a little in a casserole can make the dish very interesting. Venison concedes to its charms, and I have it on good authority that it is excellent on fried eggs.

If you like it, make a larger quantity as it keeps very well indeed.

◆

2 teaspoons dry mustard powder
2 teaspoons juice from a jar of chutney
1 pickled walnut, mashed
4 teaspoons salad oil
2 teaspoons Worcestershire sauce
2 teaspoons anchovy essence
¼–½ teaspoon chilli powder

◆

Mix all the ingredients together to form a paste.

DESSERTS

The fruits of India must have come as quite a pleasant surprise to the Memsahibs who obviously quickly become used to them, turning bananas into compotes and mangoes into brûlées and mousses. When the plains were at their hottest, the families would go to spend a few months in the hill-stations of Simla. Little bullock carts would climb up the long incline of hairpin bends loaded with fruits and vegetables. In the more temperate climate there, rose gardens flourished alongside the familiar apples, pears, blackberries, cherries, strawberries and raspberries of 'home'.

Prune Delight

◇

SERVES 4–6

 Looking through my mother-in-law's cookbook (Ceylon during the 1920s and 1930s), I was surprised to find so many prune recipes. This is one of the more unusual ones, rather like a prune summer pudding. Serve it with a big bowl of whipped cream.

◆

1 lb (450 g) prunes
juice and grated rind of 1 lemon
10 de-crusted slices white bread
4 oz (100 g) butter, melted
a handful of sultanas (optional)
4 eggs
a scant ½ pint (300 ml) milk
6 oz (175 g) caster sugar

◆

Modern-day prunes don't need soaking to the extent that the Memsahibs' prunes did. In fact, most don't need soaking at all. So start by cooking the prunes, lemon juice and rind in as little water as possible, with the lid on the pan, until the water has almost evaporated and the prunes are soft enough to be stoned. Prunes do vary so, but I doubt they will need to be cooked for more than 7–8 minutes.

Meanwhile dip your slices of bread into the melted butter and line a 2 pint (900 ml) pudding bowl with them, reserving two or three. Fill the centre with the prunes. (It wasn't in the original recipe, but I add a handful of sultanas.)

Whisk the eggs, milk and sugar together and pour over the prunes. Place the reserved pieces of bread firmly on the top. Cover tightly with two or thre layers of foil. Place the bowl in a large tin holding enough water to come about half-way up your bowl. Cook in the middle of the oven preheated to 400°F/200°C/gas 6 for 45 minutes.

This can be eaten hot, warm or cold, decanted into a serving dish deep enough to cope should it split (as can happen when served very hot).

Poor Knights of Windsor

 These early Memsahibs' recipes were very much the products of the ingredients available. Eggs were also very plentiful, and very, very small. This old English recipe pops up in many of the early books.

slices of white bread
egg
sugar
butter for frying
hot syrup
whipped cream

Start by cutting a thick slice of white bread for each person. Cut off the crusts, then cut the slice in half (or into fancy shapes for parties).

On a flat plate beat together 1 egg and 1 heaped tablespoon sugar. This amount should be enough for three slices of bread. Dip the bread in the egg mixture on both sides and fry in butter until nice and brown. Turn over and brown the under side. Serve very hot with hot syrup and whipped cream.

Mango Brûlée I

 This is a recipe from 1920, and displays much of the nostalgia for home typified by packet custard and tinned cream. Both this dish and the one following – my own – can be made with fresh or tinned mango. Peel and slice the fresh, and drain the tinned. You will need 1 medium fresh mango per person; a 14 oz (400 g) tin will feed three or four.

Make ¾ pint (450 ml) of Birds Custard as per packet. Make it fairly thick. Cool as quickly as possible and cover with clingfilm, to stop a skin forming. Place in the fridge to get as cold as possible.

Mix the cold custard with a tin of Nestlé's cream. Pour over the mango in a wide, shallow dish. Sprinkle thickly with demerara sugar and place under a very hot grill until dark and bubbly.

As it cools you will get a very nice toffee top.

Mango Brûlée II

 This is my own version. The mango part is the same as in the 1920 recipe, but after that we forget all about the custard.

Instead, whip 2 eggs into ½ pint (300 ml) double cream. Pour over the fruit in a shallow dish. Dredge with plenty of demerara sugar and place under a very hot grill. Allow the sugar to go dark and bubbling. Cool. Serve when really cold, and you have to crack the toffee on the top.

GOPAL, THE DOODWALLAH

AND even if you are one of the few who strike for independence and keep their own cow, I still counsel you to maintain amicable relations with the *Doodwallah*. One day the cow will kick and refuse to be milked, and the butler will come to you with a troubled countenance. It is a grave case and demands professional skill. The *Doodwallah* must be sent for to milk the cow. . . .

That stately man who walks up the garden path morning and evening, erect as a betel-nut palm, with a tiara of graduated milk-pots on his head, and driving a snorting buffalo before him, is Gopal himself. Scarcely any other figure in the compound impresses me in the same way as his. It is altogether Eastern in its simple dignity, and symbolically it is eloquent. The buffalo represents absolute milk and the lessening pyramid of brass *lotas*, from the great two-gallon vessel at the base to the ¼-*seer* measure at the top, stand for successive degrees of dilution with that pure element which runs in the roadside ditches after rain. Thus his insignia interpret themselves to me. Gopal does not acknowledge my heraldry, but explains that the lowest *lota* contains butter milk – that is to say, milk for making butter. The second contains milk which is excellent for drinking, but will not yield butter; the third a cheaper quality of milk for puddings, and so on. If you are an anxious mother, or a fastidious bachelor, and none of these will please you, then he brings the buffalo to the door and milks it in your presence. . . .

The "cope" is a measure like a small tea-cup, and when Gopal

has filled it, he presses the butter well down with his hand, so that a man skilled in palmistry may read the honest milkman's fortune off any cope of his butter. How he makes it, or of what materials, I dare not say. Many flavours mingle in it, some familiar enough, some unknown to me. Its texture varies too. Sometimes it is pasty, sometimes semi-fluid, sometimes sticky, following the knife. In colour it is bluish-white, unless dyed. All things considered, I refuse Gopal's butter and have mine made at home. The process is very simple, and no churn is needed. Every morning the milk for next day's butter is put into a large flat dish, to stand for twenty-four hours, at the end of which time, if the dish is as dirty as it should be, the milk has curdled. Then, with a tin spoon, Mukkun skims off the cream and puts it into a large pickle bottle, and squatting on the ground, *more suo*, bumps the bottle upon a pad until the butter is made. The artistic work of preparing it for presentation remains. First it is dyed yellow with a certain seed, that it may please the saheb's taste, for buffalo butter is quite white, and you know it is an axiom in India that cow's milk does not yield butter. Then Mukkun takes a little bamboo instrument and patiently works the butter into a "flower" and sends it to breakfast floating in cold water.   EHA

Bombay Tutti Frutti

SERVES 6–8

This recipe was given to me by a lady who remembered her mother preparing it for her in 1912, using fresh pineapple. She also remembers it being served with cream 'tinted to a delicate pink with cochineal'.

---

2 lb (900 g) apples, peeled, cored and stewed in as little water as possible, with a little sugar to taste
1 large tin pineapple chunks, drained (retain juice), or a fresh pineapple, cut into chunks
1 lb (450 g) prunes, cooked in the pineapple juice or a little water with the juice of a lemon and 4 tablespoons sugar
4 oranges, peeled, all pith removed, and then divided into segments between the membranes
1 glass brandy

Choose a pretty glass dish. Layer each fruit, aiming at two layers of each.
    Add the brandy to the remaining liquid. Pour over the fruit and chill well.

Banana Compote

◇

SERVES 6

 The Memsahibs would have encountered bananas for the first time when they arrived in India. Bananas did not travel too far afield from where they were grown until after the First World War, with the development of refrigerated ships.

◆

8–10 bananas
toasted slivered almonds (optional)

Syrup
¾ pint (450 ml) water
strips of rind from 2 limes and the juice of 1 large lime
strips of rind from and juice of 1 orange
6 oz (175 g) granulated sugar

◆

Bring all the syrup ingredients to the boil and simmer for 15–20 minutes.

Peel the bananas and cut them into diagonal chunks. Place in a wide glass dish that won't crack when the hot syrup hits it! Pour the syrup over. Sprinkle the top with slivered toasted almonds as an optional extra. Serve very cold with cream.

THE HAMAL (*and Housekeeping*)

HE next turns his attention to the books in the bookcase, and we are all familiar with his ravages there. He is usually content to bang them well with his duster, but I refer to high days, when he takes each book out and caresses it on both sides, replacing it upside down, and putting the different volumes of each work on different shelves. All this he does, not of malice, but simply because 'tis his nature to. He does not disturb the cobwebs on the corners of the bookcase, because you never told him to do so. As he moves grunting about the room the duster falls from his shoulder, and he picks it up with his toes to avoid the fatigue of stooping. When all the dusting is done, and the table-covers and ornaments are replaced, then he proceeds to shake the carpets and sweep the floor, for it is one of his ways, when left to himself, to dust first and sweep after. Finally he disposes of the rubbish which his broom has collected, by stowing it away under a cupboard, or pushing it out over the doorstep among the ferns and cal-ladiums. . . .

It was our Hamal's duty to fill the filter, and at a time when the water was very bad, orders were given that it should be boiled before being filtered. One day, my wife saw the Hamal in the act of filling the filter, and it occurred to her to warn him to let the water cool first, lest he might crack the filter. "Oh yes," said he, "I thought of that. After boiling the water, I cool it down by mixing an equal quantity of cold water with it, and then I put it into the filter." EHA

Famous Rum Omelette

◇

SERVES 2

The early Memsahibs did not dine out in hotels and restaurants because these were almost non-existent. However, if you travelled in Sri Lanka (Ceylon in those days), you made a point of stopping at certain rest-houses because they were known for particular delicacies. Here is such a one, recorded by Mrs M. G. Grandage in 1934, as served in the Sigiriya Rest-house, Ceylon.

◆

1 oz (25 g) butter
1 tablespoon soft brown sugar
3 eggs, separated
1 tablespoon rum (at least)

◆

Melt the butter and sugar in an omelette pan. Beat the egg whites until stiff, then add the yolks and beat for 5 minutes. Pour the mixture into the pan. When the mixture thickens, tip excess underneath cooked egg.

Fold over into a neat shape while nicely soft. Pour rum over omelette and set light to it. Tip on to a plate.

Bengal Coconut Crumble

SERVES 6

You don't have to be very accurate with this dish, which comes from my mother-in-law's collection. It can rely very much on what you have in your store cupboard. As a rough guide, the amount given here will feed six people.

8–10 oz (225–275g) fresh pineapple, chopped
8–10 oz (225–275 g) prunes, de-stoned and soaked overnight
4 oz (100 g) dried apricots, soaked overnight
a couple of handfuls of sultanas
3 or 4 cardamoms, crushed
8 fl oz (225 ml) white wine
8 fl oz (225 ml) water
5 oz (150 g) soft brown sugar

Crumble topping
4 oz (100 g) each of desiccated coconut, demerara sugar, butter and plain flour

---

Place all the ingredients except the topping in a large pan, and simmer for about 20 minutes. The liquid should be almost all absorbed. Pour into a pie dish.

Rub all the crumble ingredients through your fingers until they resemble breadcrumbs, then spoon over the mixture. Cook at 375°F/190°C/gas 5 until nice and brown on top.

Cashew Nut Cake

SERVES 4–6

Serve this light cake as a dessert with a separate fruit salad and a big bowl of whipped cream. It could also be served for afternoon tea – with Indian or Ceylon tea, of course!

---

4 oz (100 g) butter
4 oz (100 g) caster sugar
4 oz (100 g) cashew nuts, ground or very finely chopped
4 egg whites, whipped
a spoonful of demerara sugar

Beat the butter and sugar together until creamy. Add the nuts (keeping a spoonful to one side) and the flour. Fold in the well beaten egg whites.

Pour into a well buttered spring-form tin lined with a disc of equally well buttered greaseproof paper. Cook for 30 minutes in a preheated oven at 375°F/190°C/gas 5.

Sprinkle the top with the remaining nuts and the demerara sugar, and cook for 15 more minutes.

Allow to cool before removing from the tin. If it has stuck firmly to the paper, leave it on, but don't forget it when you serve the cake!

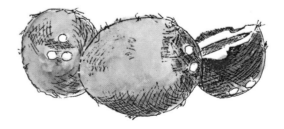

THE MEMSAHIB'S SECRETS

SOME helpful hints for the Memsahib from a cookbook by 'Hausfrau' published in 1913, by A. M. & J. Ferguson, Colombo.

◆

The ends of candles melted down with a little turpentine make a very good floor polish.

◆

The juice of half a lime in a cup of black coffee without any sugar is a good remedy for a headache.

◆

When boiling eggs, wet the shells with cold water before dropping into boiling water. They will never crack.

◆

A few drops of glycerine in cold water will stop hiccoughs.

◆

A dessertspoon of cold water beaten up with each egg white will double the quantity.

◆

A little ground almonds mixed through a fruit cake will prevent the fruit sinking to the bottom.

◆

To prevent moths, sprinkle clothes with either peppercorns or cayenne pepper.

◆

To clean silver filigree ornaments, make a thin paste of cream of tartar and cold water and spread thickly. Cover and leave for about 4 days. Rinse with warm soapy water.

◆

A little white sugar in the water in which green vegetables are boiled will preserve their colour.

———◆———

Tea leaves are excellent for cleaning decanters.

———◆———

When stewing fruit, add the sugar after the fruit has been cooked but while it is still hot. A lot less sugar is needed.

———◆———

If breadcrumbs are not handy for frying, try a little semolina instead.

———◆———

Instead of eggs, glaze pastry with a little caster sugar in milk.

———◆———

Ink stains can be removed by rubbing with ripe tomato.

———◆———

Skipping before a warm bath is about the best exercise a woman can take when she is inclined to stoutness.

———◆———

How to make yeast: juice of 2 limes mixed with 2 tablespoons flour and 2 tablespoons sugar and 1 cup hot water. Bottle until needed.

———◆———

If a lime is warmed before it is squeezed it will give double the juice.

———◆———

Clean amber by rubbing it with olive oil.

———◆———

When boiling old potatoes add a little milk to the water and they will not go black.

Remedy for a Cold

 This recipe is by courtesy of a colonel's lady!

'It should cure anything. Even if it doesn't – it will certainly ensure you die happy!

◆

6 oz Best Jamaica Rum
6 oz Fresh Lime Juice
4 oz Honey
3 oz Olive Oil

◆

Mix well together & shake the bottle before each dose.

THE DOSE:– 1 tablespoon every three or four hours. Oftener if the cold is very severe.'

The honey and oil soothe the throat.
The lime soothes the stomach.
The rum soothes you!

THAT DHOBIE!

'A PUPPY rending slippers, a child tearing up its picture books, a mungoose killing twenty chickens to feed on one, a free-thinker demolishing ancient superstitions, what are they all but *Dhobies* in embryo? . . . the *Dhobie*, dashing your cambric and fine linen against the stones, shattering a button, fraying a hem, or rending a seam at every stroke, feels a triumphant con-tempt for the miserable creature whose plodding needle and thread put the garment together . . . Day after day he has stood before that great black stone and wreaked his rage upon shirt and trowser and coat, and coat and trowser and shirt. Then he has wrung them as if he were wringing the necks of poultry, and fixed them on his drying lines with thorns and spikes, and finally he has taken the battered garments to his torture chamber and ploughed them with his iron, longwise and crosswise and slantwise, and dropping glowing cinders on their tenderest places. Son has followed father through countless generations in cultivating this passion for destruction. . . . Indeed, I sometimes find that, while he has successfully wrecked the garment, he has overlooked the dirt!

. . . Next morning when you spring from your tub and shake out the great jail towel which is to wrap your shivering person in its warm folds, lo! it yawns from end to end. There is nothing but a border, a fringe, left. You fling on your clothes in ususual haste, for it is mail day morning. The most indispensible of them all has scarcely a remnant of a button remaining. You snatch up another which seems in better condition, and scramble into it; but, in the course of the day, a cold current of wind, penetrating where it ought not, makes you aware of what your friends behind you back have noticed for some time, *viz.*, that the starch with which a gaping rent had been carefully gummed together, that you might not see it, has melted and given way.　EHA

SOME VOCABULARY

SO many words in everyday use come from India. You shop in a *bazaar* for *pyjamas*, *bandannas*, *bangles*, and perhaps a few *cheroots*. When you get home to your *bungalow*, you may sit on your *verandah* and have a drink of *punch*. If there is a *gymkhana* that day you will need to don your *jodhpurs* which are probably *khaki*. Your clothes would be made of *seersucker*, *calico* or *chintz*, or you may wear *dungarees* or a *shawl*. For *tiffin*, you might use sugar *tongs* or serve *chutney*. Then there is *chit, cot, chum, dinghy, loot, yoga, pundit, kedgeree, thug*. We talk about '*all that gup*' (gossip). A *godown* is a store where you buy all sorts of goods, but hopefully you won't *get a crab* (tummy ache). If things *go phut* you can cheer yourself with either a *peg* of whisky or a cup of *char*!

Not forgetting *posh*, thought to be derived from the best way of travelling by ship to and from India (*p*ort *o*ut *s*tarboard *h*ome).

GLOSSARY

ASAFOETIDA – a strong smelling sour spice.

BAY LEAF – powdered, it gives a very distinctive flavour – excellent with chicken or pork.

BOMBAY DUCK – dried fish. Either crisp in the oven or under the grill. Break into small pieces and serve as a side dish.

CARDAMOM – aromatic. Crush seed pod before putting into your curry.

CORIANDER – fry seeds in oil or butter and add to vegetables. Ground coriander is lovely in stews.

CREAMED COCONUT – buy in small packets. Add chunks to soup and curries for ultra-rich flavour.

CUMIN Good for a tummy-ache!

CURRY LEAF – fresh leaf from a small shrub – very hard to get.

CURRY PASTE – bought in jars. We prefer Fern's curry paste. A very small amount (a teaspoon) in a casserole will give a delightful flavour and aroma without being "hot".

DESICCATED COCONUT – pour boiling water over dry coconut. Stir and leave 15 minutes – squeeze out milk and use in curry dishes. Coconut itself is used as a side dish.

FENUGREEK – marvellous aroma. Too much fenugreek can make a curry bitter and sickly . . . be sparing.

GHEE – a strong flavoured butter originally made from buffalo's milk. Now made from Indian cow's milk and available in tins.

LIMES – use in preference to lemons.

ROOT GINGER – peel and chop into small pieces.

TAMARIND – the fruit of a large tree – pod tangy and sharp. Pour boiling water over fruit and then sieve to remove pips. Very piquant.

TURMERIC – a bright yellow powder that can be used instead of saffron.

YOGHURT – the ideal liquid to cook your curries in.

INDEX

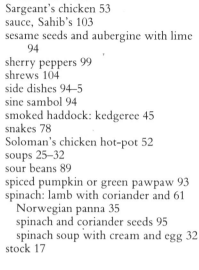